THEOLOGICAL
METHOD IN
JACQUES ELLUL

Daniel B. Clendenin

UNIVERSITY
PRESS OF
AMERICA

Lanham • New York • London

Copyright © 1987 by

University Press of America,® Inc.

4720 Boston Way
Lanham, MD 20706

3 Henrietta Street
London WC2E 8LU England

British Cataloging in Publication Information Available

Library of Congress Cataloging-in-Publication Data

Clendenin, Daniel B.
 Theological method in Jacques Ellul.

 Bibliography: p.
 Includes index.
 1. Ellul, Jacques. I. Title.
BX4827.E5C54   1987   230'.42'0924   87-10506
ISBN 0-8191-6427-5 (alk. paper)
ISBN 0-8191-6428-3 (pbk. : alk. paper)

The author gratefully acknowledges permission to reprint the following:

Excerpts from In Season, Out of Season, by Jacques Ellul; translated by Lani K. Niles, San Francisco: Harper and Row, 1982. Permission granted by Le Centurion, Paris, France.

Portions from pages 15-18; 43; 56-59; 67; 75-79; 81-82; 88; 134; 175; 181; 183; 186; 188-190; 193-195; 201-203; 206-208; 211-212; and 219-220.

Excerpts from, "Will the Real Ellul Please Stand Up? A Bibliographic Survey," by Daniel B. Clendenin in The Trinity Journal 6 NS (1985): 167-183.

DEDICATION

To Patty, <u>mon   petit chou</u>, whose constant love and
encouragement reflect only a small portion of the immeasurable
influence she has had on my life, I dedicate this work.

THEOLOGICAL METHOD IN JACQUES ELLUL

Table of Contents

For the past several years I have read and reread the bulk of Jacques Ellul's corpus, a task which I have found to be humbling, unwieldy, and enriching. The completion of the present work caused me to appreciate anew Calvin's note to his readers, actually a quotation from Saint Augustine, in his 1559 Institutes: "I count myself one of the number of those who write as they learn and learn as they write."

Several factors complicate Ellul interpretation. First, the size of his project is not only vast (over 40 books and 800-plus articles), and still increasing, but also wide-ranging. Ellul the polymath commands an encyclopedic competence in not one but many fields: history, law, sociology, politics, and theology. Tackling the secondary literature can prove even more frustrating, for there one encounters radically diverse interpretations in which both praise and damnation spring from all quarters, both left and right.

In addition, failure to note the explicit purpose or goal which Ellul hopes to achieve with his reader almost always results in lopsided conclusions which brand him as a pessimistic naysayer. Like Kierkegaard, Ellul has described himself as a doctor who has the unpleasant but necessary task of diagnosing an illness. This is the first step towards health, a negative critique which scrutinizes the commonly accepted but facile prognosis, and it is Ellul's specialty. Thus, in another place, Ellul styles himself "a troublemaker, or creator of uncertainty," by which he means something like the role of a Socratic gadfly who shakes us from deadly slumber and lethargy. If Ellul seems to say precious little that is positive and constructive, we need to remember that it is not his initial purpose, nor can it be, given his analysis of current conditions. Add to all of this his peculiar writing style, with its propensity to hyperbole and heated rhetoric, and one begins to appreciate the frustrations which interpreters sometimes encounter.

The purpose of the present work is to dispel some of the negative effects of the above factors by suggesting that Ellul's theological method revolves around one key theme or kernel idea, the dialectical interplay between freedom and necessity. This one key theme appears as a golden thread which winds its way through all of his works, and which serves as a sort of hermeneutical key to his thinking. Thus, Chapters One and Two present some necessary introductory matters, while Chapters Three and Four explicate the main thesis. In Chapter Five, I conclude with some strengths and weaknesses in Ellul's method.

Many people contributed to the final completion of this project, and while any weaknesses are all my own, it is my pleasure to acknowledge their help. Pieter de Jong, David W. Gill, Tom Hanks, David G. Lalka, Craig Mayes, James H. Pain, and my lovely wife, Patty, all read the complete manuscript and offered constructive criticisms. Joyce Hanks provided me with hard-to-find French articles by and about Ellul, and that with exceptional speed and kindness. Martha Clendenin, Robert Collesano, Richard and Margie Pierce, Flemming and Cindy Rose, Dorothy Payne Wood, and William Tyndale College provided financial assistance. Bill Shoemaker and Herb Cocking of William Tyndale College encouraged me to complete the project, despite its detracting me from classroom duties. Shari Benscoter typed the final manuscript. Special thanks go to Hank French and Don Thorsen for their insight, wit and friendship, all of which provoke me still.

DBC
William Tyndale College
Easter, 1987

Tertullian's famous throwing down of the gauntlet, "What does Athens have to do with Jerusalem?," could be (and in fact was) answered in several different ways. At the most basic level, biblical faith is intrinsically monotheistic and wholistic. There is one God, Lord of all of life -- Athenian philosophy as well as Jerusalem piety. In our own century of intellectual fragmentation and ferment, "What does sociology have to do with theology?" and "What do laity have to do with the theological guild?" are among the "Tertullianic" challenges deserving careful response.

Daniel Clendenin's study of theological method in Jacques Ellul is a helpful and stimulating examination of one of the 20th century's most powerful and original thinkers. Although Jacques Ellul carried out an ambitious program of theological studies with the Strasbourg theological faculty during World War Two (when both Ellul and that faculty were forced to a harried existence in southern France), he has always been a true layman, working as a social historian and sociologist and not as professional pastor or theologian. Ellul's theology emerges less from questions raised by other professional theologians than the tensions, challenges and possibilities of a thoughtful Christian deeply engaged in the secular world. This alone is adequate reason (in our specialized, professionalized era) for giving Ellul a careful hearing.

But Ellul is also a sociologist -- many of us would say the "premier" social critic and analyst of modern technological society. Theologians often respectfully dabble in the social sciences; Ellul is a sociologist who (much more than) "dabbles" in theology in more than twenty books. What does sociology have to do with theology? First, there is a dialectical interplay between the two approaches. One attempts a scientific description and analysis of this-worldly reality; the other attempts a careful hearing and formulation of divine, revelational truth. Christian existence takes place at the living, ever-renewed intersection of truth and reality. Second, both within sociology and within theology, dialectic is characteristic of the domain of study. Daniel Clendenin's choice of the dialectic of freedom and necessity as the focal point of Ellul's theological method is right on target. As becomes clear in reading the present study, however, it is the same dialectic of freedom and necessity that, in different expressions, is also the key to Ellul's sociological method.

Clendenin's study reinforces my own conviction that Ellul's theological contribution is simultaneously a powerful challenge, corrective, and even an antidote to contemporary Evangelical,

Liberal, and Liberation theologies. This is so, first of all, because of his creative loyalty to the Word of God in Scripture and Jesus Christ. The Word must be free to act and to question us and our categories or assumptions. Neither a lukewarm drifting away from biblical authority nor an ideological freezing or self-serving exploitation of Scripture will do in our rudderless era. Second, Ellul's provocative, learned social analysis is essential in a politicized environment prone to naive justifications of Marxist, Liberal, or Conservative agendas. In short, Ellul drives us to follow him and, still more, improve upon him by planting our theological feet firmly in the truth of the Word of God and in a realistic social analysis.

To understand Ellul (or any powerful, prolific thinker), one must first enter his thought world with a pound of respect and openness, a few ounces of passion, and a ton of dedication, energy, and hard work. Daniel Clendenin has done this in admirable fashion, emerging as a critical, constructive voice in his own right. His own American Evangelical theological fraternity is thereby enriched and all who are interested in the various crises and questions of contemporary theology will be assisted.

David W. Gill
Professor of Christian Ethics
New College Berkeley
Berkeley, California
World Communion Sunday, October 5, 1986

INTRODUCTION

With over 40 books and 800 articles, Jacques Ellul,
recently retired professor from the University of Bordeaux,
ranks as one of the most prolific scholars of today. In
addition to this sheer quantity of scholarship, Ellul brings to
the theological task a freshness and creativity which invites a
critical engagement with his thought. It is not without reason
that Martin Marty refers to him as the one person he would
recommend as able to inform the church of its proper agenda.[1]

It is not surprising that Ellul's work has met with mixed
reviews. It is an overstatement, though, as we shall show in
the first chapter, to suggest that his work has been overlooked
or that there is a dearth of secondary literature about Ellul.
This is true only in a limited sense in that there are currently
only five books given to Ellul study, and three of these are
collections of essays. Further, what has been written about
Ellul varies widely in its seriousness and dependability as
scholarship. On the other hand, Ellul has not been neglected,
in spite of his own complaints to that effect. Joyce Hanks'
recently published Jacques Ellul: A Comprehensive Bibliography
(1984) explodes the misconception that Ellul is overlooked as a
scholar. She documents over 1200 secondary pieces written about
Ellul and is already working on a supplement which is due for
publication in 1987. Thus, while it is clear that Ellul has not
been entirely neglected, it is not certain that the true nature
and goal of his work is understood by everyone.

The purpose of this book is to help correct some of the
many misreadings of Ellul and to foster the ongoing dialogue
with his work through a critical examination of his theological
method. Since no one has treated this topic at length, the
project hopes to make an original contribution. In the
extensive subject index of Hanks' bibliography, for example,
there is no entry pertaining to Ellul's theological method. The
work, therefore, helps to fill a recognized void in scholarship
on an important aspect of a prolific theological scholar. It
also hopes to contribute to the ongoing discussion about theological method in general.

The method employed to carry out this purpose varies
slightly with each chapter. Chapters One and Two are analytic
and descriptive. Chapters Three and Four, in which I propose an

---

[1]Martin Marty, on the back cover of the dust jacket of
Ellul's The Ethics of Freedom.

original hermeneutical key to Ellul's thought, are more synthetic and interpretive. Chapter Five comprises my own critical interaction with Ellul's theological method. There I propose what I see as some of the strengths and weaknesses in Ellul. Throughout the entire book I occasionally draw upon biographical material to illustrate, complement and explain certain aspects of Ellul. This biographical method is not unimportant, either, for more than in many writers, Ellul's writings are based in his personal experiences. This, in fact, is a calculated tactic on his part: to write about his experiences.

A simple illustration of concentric circles helps to illustrate the relation and progression of the five chapters. Chapter One represents the largest, outer circle, for it is the broadest in scope. There I propose a typology of methodological perspectives by which interpreters have read Ellul. A survey of the secondary literature reveals that people variously read Ellul as a theological positivist, existentialist, prophet, and dialectician. In this first chapter I show the extent to which these descriptions are or are not applicable to Ellul's theological method and then draw some conclusions about what I call his "eclecticism."

Chapter Two represents an inner, more narrow circle. Here I focus on just one methodological perspective, the idea that Ellul is best understood as a dialectician. After a brief overview of the confused history of the term "dialectics," I locate Ellul in theology's own use of this method, examine what he himself has said on this, and illustrate how this works out in his writings. I suggest that Ellul's dialectical method operates as a description of reality, an epistemological orientation to understand this reality, and as a Biblical-theological framework by which to read the Bible and craft a peculiarly Christian style of life.

Chapters Three and Four, which comprise something of a single unit, represent the innermost of the three concentric circles. There I focus attention on one particular aspect of Ellul's dialectic, the dialectical relationship of freedom and necessity. This particular dialectic, I suggest, forms the golden thread which runs throughout all of Ellul's work. That is, it is the constituent element or underlying theme of all he has written. Understanding this one particular dialectical relationship helps to understand the direction of Ellul's overall corpus. Chapter Three examines the first pole of the dialectic, necessity, while Chapter Four examines the second pole, freedom.

Chapter Five steps back once again in order to get the big picture and to interact in a critical fashion with the material

results of the first four chapters. After providing a short
review and some preliminary conclusions, I suggest four criticisms and three strengths of Ellul's theological method. I do
not propose that Ellul's method is by itself complete or even
entirely consistent. In fact, I think it is true that some of
his strengths turn out to be weaknesses. At any rate, Ellul
himself would argue that it is epistemologically inappropriate
and naive to imagine that any single method or approach to the
truth is the one, exclusive and best way.[2] In the words of
Ellul scholar David W. Gill, who is probably the most able of
American interpreters of the prophet from Bordeaux, I conclude
that it is most profitable to go through Ellul, but that it is
also necessary to go beyond him.[3]

---

[2]This was his problem with Calvin's orientation, the
suggestion that Calvin alone was right. See In Season, Out of
Season, pp. 17-18.

[3]David Gill, The Word of God in the Ethics of Jacques
Ellul, p. 156.

CHAPTER ONE

MAPPING THE TERRAIN:
A SURVEY OF THE ELLUL LITERATURE

...l'activité intellectuelle du Pr. Ellul est aujourd'hui plus intense que jamais et il donne à une échelle plus vaste ce qu'il réserva longtemps à quelques privilégiés. Cet hommage ne marque qu'un moment d'une vie qui parvient à son plein épanouissement.

Dmitri Georges Lavroff
Président de l'Université de Bordeaux.[1]

A. Introduction

Gone is the time when scholars such as Clifford Christians and Jay M. Van Hook, the Ellul experts who edited Jacques Ellul: Interpretive Essays, could write that "surprisingly little serious analysis, interpretation and criticism of [Ellul's] work has appeared in print."[2] Equally anachronistic is Waldo Beach's suggestion that Ellul remains "relatively unknown to American readers,"[3] an appraisal which even Ellul complained of as recently as 1982.[4]

---

[1]Dmitri Georges Lavroff, "Avant-propos," in Religion, société et politique: Mélanges en hommage à Jacques Ellul, eds. Etienne Dravasa, Claude Emeri, and Jean-Louis Seurin (Paris: Presses Universitaires de France, 1983), p. x.

[2]Clifford G. Christians and Jay M. Van Hook, eds., Jacques Ellul: Interpretive Essays (Urbana: University of Illinois Press, 1981), p. xi. Hereafter cited as JE:IE.

[3]Waldo Beach, "Forward," in To Will and to Do, trans. C. Edward Hopkin, by Jacques Ellul (Philadelphia: Pilgrim Press, 1969), p. vi.

[4]Jacques Ellul, In Season, Out of Season, trans. Lani K. Niles (San Francisco: Harper and Row, 1982), pp. 193-194. Hereafter cited as ISOS. Compare Ellul's similar remarks in "Mirror of These Ten Years," The Christian Century 87 (February 18, 1970): 202. Two Europeans once told Stephen Rose that "Ellul was just a frustrated man who had never been 'accepted' and who spent most of his time railing against the fact." See "Whither Ethics, Jacques Ellul?" in James Y. Holloway, ed. Introducing Jacques Ellul (Grand Rapids: Eerdmans, 1970), p. 129.

1

Not a dearth of literature but a near avalanche more accurately characterizes the current state of Ellul research. As one professor recently remarked to me, Ellul's corpus has spawned a virtual industry of scholarship. Joyce Hanks' newly published Jacques Ellul: A Comprehensive Bibliography (1984) bears this out. In addition to Ellul's 40 books and 600 articles, she documents over 750 reviews of Ellul's books, 17 interviews, 20 theses and dissertations, and nearly 300 "books, articles, and notices."[5] The would-be interpreter of Ellul, then, faces not a mole hill but a mountain of secondary literature.

Quantity need not indicate quality, of course, as anyone who has begun to scale the mountain can verify. Some of the work is perceptive, while some of it simply perpetuates misinformation.[6] Some scholars exhibit an eye for Ellul's sophistication and nuance, while others are blatantly polemical and partisan. If reading Ellul himself is difficult, as Wilkinson and Outka, for example, lament,[7] reading his interpreters may prove even more difficult. This Ellul industry has churned out a bewildering confusion of contradictory and divergent caricatures of the professor from Bordeaux, with the consequence that "he is too easily misunderstood."[8] While

---

[5]Joyce Hanks, Research in Philosophy and Technology. Supplement 1. Jacques Ellul: A Comprehensive Bibliography (Greenwich, C.T.: JAI Press, 1984), pp. 139-221. Hanks has completed a supplementary volume which updates this bibliography and is due for publication in March, 1987.

[6]Paul Pickerel, for example, in his very favorable review of Ellul's The Technological Society, referred to Ellul as "a Catholic layman." Ellul has never been a Catholic. Unfortunately, the label was printed on the back cover of the 1964 American edition of The Technological Society. For Pickerel's article, see "Heading Toward Postcivilization (Boulder, Berkner, Ellul, Snow, Murdoch, Bellow)" Harper's Magazine 229 (October 1964): 124.

[7]As Wilkinson put it so well, "The major problem in writing an introduction to any work of Ellul is...to persuade sensible people not to throw it down before they have negotiated even the first ten pages." See his "Introduction" in Ellul's The Meaning of the City, trans. Dennis Pardee (Grand Rapids: Eerdmans, 1970), p. xii. Cf. Outka's similar frustration in his article "Discontinuity in Ellul's Ethics," in JE:IE, p. 216.

[8]Darrell Fasching, The Thought of Jacques Ellul: A Systematic Exposition (New York: Edwin Mellen Press, 1981) p. viii.

Christians and Van Hook are outdated in their suggestion to imply a lack of Ellul literature, Fasching may well be correct to insist that, notwithstanding this quantity of work, "the nature and results of Jacques Ellul's work are very largely misunderstood."[9]

A cursory sampling of the secondary literature illustrates this confusion. We read there that Ellul is "the quintessential Protestant of his time,"[10] a Catholic layman,[11] a "conservative evangelical" and a "biblical conservative,"[12] a theologian rejected by "conservative Christians,"[13] a Calvinist,[14] one whose thought is "quite foreign to the mind and spirit of Calvin,"[15] an uncompromising Barthian,[16] the opposite of

---

[9]Ibid. Gary Wren makes the same point in his dissertation, "Technique, Society, and Politics: A Critical Study of the Work of Jacques Ellul" (PhD dissertation, Claremont Graduate School, 1977), p. 2, when he observes the "almost universal distortion" and "ingenious oversimplification" of Ellul's work.

[10]Martin Marty, "Introduction: Creative Misuses of Jacques Ellul," in JE:IE, p. 14.

[11]Paul Pickerel, ibid.

[12]Waldo Beach, ibid. Thomas Hanks suggests that this designation is a misnomer. See his article "How Ellul Transcends Liberation Theologies," TSF Bulletin (September-October 1984):13.

[13]Christopher Walters-Bugbee, "The Politics of Revelation," Sojourners (June 1977): 6-7. He rightly shows, though, how those of the "left," both politically and theologically, scorn Ellul.

[14]Numerous people level this charge, as we shall show below. As one example, see Randall H. Ihara, "Redeeming the Time: Theology, Technology, and Politics in the Thought of Jacques Ellul" (PhD dissertation, University of Tennessee, 1975-76), pp. vi-vii.

[15]Lester DeKoster, Banner (July 16, 1971): 24-25.

[16]Stephen Rose, "Whither Ethics, Jacques Ellul?" in James Y. Holloway, ed. Introducing Jacques Ellul (Grand Rapids: Eerdmans, 1970), p. 124.

Barth at places,[17] a pessimist and fatalist,[18] an apocalyp-
ticist,[19] a utopian,[20] a person who has dismissed Marx and
who is unacquainted with his writings,[21] and a scholar who with
an unparalleled knowledge of Marx serves as the true precursor
of liberation theology.[22] In a near-comical understatement,
Thomas Hanks writes that "it is difficult for the scholars of
the north to pigeonhole Jacques Ellul."[23] It is obvious that
one can find what he is looking for and thus neatly label Ellul
in the desired manner.

---

[17]Gabriel Vahanian, "Jacques Ellul and the Religious
Illusion," in The Thought of Jacques Ellul: A Systematic Exposition, p. xviii. Vahanian's article first appeared in the book
Mélanges en hommage à Jacques Ellul, cited in footnote #1 of
this chapter.

[18]Again, this charge is ubiquitous. As an example, see
Lewis Mumford, The Myth of the Machine, II (New York: Harcourt,
Brace, and World, 1964), pp. 290-291. Victor Ferkiss is also
often cited in this regard.

[19]Gabriel Vahanian, "Technology, Politics, and the
Christian Faith," in Introducing Jacques Ellul, p. 60.

[20]Fasching, pp. x-xi, 172-173, and 188-189.

[21]Christopher Lasch, "The Social Thought of Jacques
Ellul," in Introducing Jacques Ellul, p. 88, footnote #2. David
John Burke makes a similar remark, saying that "Ellul's thought
bears little resemblance to Marx." See his "Jacques Ellul:
Theologian and Social Critic" (PhD dissertation, Washington
State University, 1980), p. 134.

[22]Thomas Hanks, "Jacques Ellul: The Original Liberation
Theologian," TSF Bulletin (May-June 1984):8. In a footnote in
his book Autopsy of Revolution, Ellul actually claims that he
was the first "liberation theologian." See p. 218, footnote #23
of that book.

[23]Ibid. Katharine Temple makes the same point in her
dissertation vis-à-vis Ellul's sociological method, which,
according to her, "does not fit easily into standard categories."
See her "The Task of Jacques Ellul: A Proclamation of Biblical
Faith as Requisite for Understanding the Modern Project" (PhD
dissertation, McMaster University, Hamilton, Ontario, 1976),
p. 168.

This chapter attempts to synthesize the major secondary work on Ellul in order to outline and analyze the methodological categories used to interpret him, locate various influences on his thought, and to acquaint the reader with the current state of Ellul research. While this bibliographic essay cannot even come close to being exhaustive, the hope is that no major works or interpretive categories have been overlooked. Having accomplished this bibliographic task, we are in a better position to focus our attention on the exact nature of Ellul's method. To facilitate the goal of this chapter I have created a typology to categorize the major interpretive approaches to Ellul. The four types are Ellul as a theological positivist, an existentialist, a prophet, and a dialectician. The chapter concludes with a review of the advances made in Ellul research.

B. Ellul as a Theological Positivist

One perspective from which to read Ellul is to insist that his methodology is that of a "theological positivist," a term which Ihara borrows from John Cobb in order to describe Ellul.[24] By "positivist" Ihara seems to imply two things: one whose methodology "is a brand of neo-Reformation Protestantism,"[25] and which has "a certain conception of reason."[26] Ihara tells us little more about this second aspect except to suggest that it involves a separation between reason and faith which affirms the ultimate sovereignty of the latter over the former. Other positivists, he suggests, include Barth and Kierkegaard. Both of these points could be affirmed about Ellul. On the one hand, as a member of the Reformed Church of France, Ellul is indeed "reformed." In addition, one need only read such a work as his Living Faith to appreciate his stress on the priority of

---

[24]Ihara, pp. 44-46. Ihara footnotes John Cobb's Living Options in Protestant Theology: A Survey of Methods (Philadelphia: Westminster Press, 1962). As I will attempt to show, although Cobb's category of theological positivism might well apply to Ellul, his third category of theological existentialism, which Ihara does not mention, might apply to Ellul equally well.

[25]Ibid., p. vi.

[26]Ibid., p. 52. Both Ihara (p. 57) and Temple (entire chapter III) point out that Ellul is not opposed to reason, but that he wants to relegate it to its proper sphere and to avoid what he sees as a sort of epistemological hubris.

5

revelation over reason.[27] Yet problems begin when, as many do, people begin to equate this with Calvinism, and Ellul as a Calvinist.[28]

1. Ellul and Calvin

Much of the secondary literature describes Ellul as a Calvinist, a label which is not only sufficiently vague, but simply misleading when applied to Ellul. At one time he read Calvin and was influenced by him, but today his theology has developed and gone far beyond the Genevan Reformer. Granted, the two thinkers emphasize some common theological themes, like the falleness of man, God as Wholly Other, the authority of Scripture, the "humble use of right reason,"[29] and so on, but is this tantamount to Calvinism? Could not a non-Calvinist affirm these points? The operative assumption seems to be the non-sequitur that since Ellul is French and belongs to a reformed denomination, he must, therefore, be a Calvinist.

Matheke suggests, for example, that Ellul's work represents "a reappropriation of the Reformation insights for our time... directly in the tradition of Martin Luther and John Calvin."[30] Heddendorf writes that Ellul is "consistently and doggedly

---

[27]Jacques Ellul, Living Faith: Belief and Doubt in a Perilous World, trans. Peter Heinegg (San Francisco: Harper and Row, 1983), part I. See especially the dialogue between Monos and Una, the entire chapter 16. Another good example of Ellul's "positive" methodology would be his explicit rejection of natural theology, seen, for example, in his book The Theological Foundation of Law.

[28]For an excellent treatment of the history of the terms "positivism," "positive theology," and "theological positivism," see Wolfhart Pannenberg, Theology and the Philosophy of Science, trans. Francis McDonagh (Philadelphia: Westminster Press, 1976), especially Chapter One, pp. 242-249, and 265-275.

[29]Temple, p. 121.

[30]David Matheke, "To Will and To Do God's Word: An Examination of the Christian Meaning of the Works of Jacques Ellul" (D.Div. thesis, Vanderbilt Divinity School, 1972), p. 4. With its pearl-stringing of Ellul quotes, numerous misspellings, typographical errors, improper footnotations, poor grammar and total lack of any criticism, Matheke's thesis was disappointing.

Reformed."[31]   Ihara goes on to   argue   that   Ellul's   thought   is
particularly   indebted   to   "his   own   updated   version   of   the
teachings of John Calvin   and   his   followers,"[32]   and   that   his
"controversial   theses   on   theology and   politics   can   only be
understood in relation to his understanding of the   teachings   of
Calvin"[33] and to "his brand of Calvinism."[34]

Most   disconcerting   is H.T. Wilson's article which perpetuates misinformation about   Ellul's   "Calvinism."[35]   Contrary   to
what   Wilson   claims,   Ellul   has   never   "describe[d] himself as a
French   Calvinist."[36]   Ellul   was   not   "raised   a   Catholic,"[37]
nor   does   he ever mention a "conversion to Calvinism."[38]   "Ellul
the Calvinist"[39] does not "dissuade Christians   from   involvement
in   the   world."[40]   Further,   he   does   not attack "all forms of
social action" as   a   "restatement   of   the   faith   _versus_   works
controversy   so   central   to Luther's, but especially to Calvin's

----

[31]Russell   Heddendorf,   "The   Christian   World   of   Jacques
Ellul,"   Christian   Scholar's   Review,   vol.   2,   no.   4   (1973):
291-307.

[32]Ihara, p. 52.   He quotes from   H.T.   Wilson.   See   below,
footnote #35.

[33]Ibid., p. 320.

[34]Ibid., p. 330.

[35]H.T.   Wilson,   "The   Sociology   of   Apocalypse: Jacques
Ellul's   Reformation   of   Reformation   Thought,"   Human   Context,
vol. 7, no. 3 (1975): 474-494.

[36]Ibid.,   p.   474.   Wilson   footnotes   Ellul's introduction
to Holloway's Introducing Jacques Ellul,   "From   Jacques   Ellul,"
to   substantiate   this   and   the   following   point   about Ellul's
Catholic upbringing, yet Ellul never even comes close   to   saying
any of these things in the text cited.

[37]Ibid.

[38]Ibid.

[39]Ibid., p. 477.

[40]Ibid., p. 486.   Quite the opposite is true, in fact.

7

reformation."[41]   Likewise   erroneous   are   William   Kuhns's
remarks   that   "the determinism, the unflagging idealism, and the
sober, urgent mood of The Technological Society have more than a
little to do with his [Ellul's] stance as a militant Christian
Calvinist...[T]here can be little question that Ellul's staunch
Calvinism has profoundly affected his sociology."[42]   These
gross generalizations show little acquaintance with the true
nature of Ellul's thought.

Ellul   propounds   a   host   of doctrines which, to use Lester
DeKoster's words, are "quite foreign to the mind and spirit of
Calvin."[43]   His   rigorous affirmation of the universal salvation
of all people, that "it is not theologically possible that there
be damned men,"[44]   would be repugnant to Calvin. As for his
conception of the doctrine of salvation, he suggests that the
traditional-Biblical   idea of slavery to sin and redemption from
it have other modern equivalents in the quasi-Marxian ideas of
alienation and liberation.[45]   He casts the Christian life in
terms of one's "freedom won in Christ, [which] is alive,
unlimited, without restrictions or obligations,"[46] a mindset
hard to reconcile with Calvin's famed tertius usus of the Law
and   rigorous   self-denial.[47]   Ellul   categorically rejects

---

[41]Ibid., p. 485. One could argue, I think, that Calvin
is more often accused of a type of ascetic, works righteousness,
and that Luther was much more concerned that works righteousness
would usurp his doctrines of faith alone and the freedom of a
Christian.

[42]William Kuhns, The Post-Industrial Prophets (New York:
Weybright and Talley, 1971), p. 84.

[43]DeKoster, ibid.

[44]Jacques   Ellul,   Apocalypse; The Book of Revelation,
trans. George Schreiner (New York: Seabury, 1977), p. 214.
Hereafter cited as Apocalypse. See Ellul's footnote #15 on
pages 275-276 where he expounds on this topic.   For further
references to his universalism, see ISOS, pp. 58, 75-76, 134,
and 211-212.

[45]Idem, The Ethics of Freedom, trans. Geoffrey Bromiley
(Grand Rapids: Eerdmans, 1976), pp. 49, 66-67.

[46]Ibid., p. 186.

[47]I have in mind here Calvin's exposition of the Christian
life as he expounds it in III.vi-x. of his Institutes. In fact,
Ellul's definition of the Christian life just cited might apply
more readily to Luther.

natural theology, whereas reputable Calvin scholars such as Dowey, Brunner, and Warfield make a case that Calvin affirmed it. [48] Ellul's ideas on the state differ from Calvin, too. He does not make religious freedom the _sine_ _qua_ _non_ of good government as Calvin does.[49]

Likewise, some of Calvin's doctrines would be repugnant to Ellul, including his doctrine of predestination and his doctrine of a highly structured church (in contrast to Ellul's reputed individualism). Finally, whereas Calvin might be portrayed as the system-builder _par_ _excellence_, Ellul expresses a profound distaste for any systematizing.[50]

In conclusion, then, it is mystifying how some scholars persist in describing Ellul as "a lay theologian who mirrors the deep Calvinism of his French Reformed Church."[51] Ellul himself, for those who care to listen to him, clearly explains: "I am not a Calvinist, and even though Calvin's writing influenced me some time ago, I have since moved away, quite far even, from his position."[52]

---

[48]Other Calvin scholars, of course, deny that Calvin affirms any sort of natural theology. Those would include Barth, Niesel, Parker, and T.F. Torrance. At any rate, if the issue is unclear in Calvin, it is not unclear in Ellul.

[49]Ellul, The Ethics of Freedom, p. 435: "It is odd that religious freedom has often been advanced as a definition of good government, even in Calvin and Barth."

[50]Idem, ISOS, p. 203.

[51]"Review of The Meaning of the City by Jacques Ellul," Time, December 7, 1970, p. 56. Even Jay M. VanHook, one of the editors of the book JE:IE, falls into this same mistake when, in his article in the book, p. 136, he refers to Ellul's "roots in the tradition of French Calvinism." One final example of this misconception is Gary Wren's otherwise excellent doctoral dissertation, in which he contends that Ellul's break with the Personalist Movement "might be seen as a reassertion of his individualistic Calvinism" (p. 48).

[52]Ellul, ISOS, pp. 57-58. See also pp. 16-18, 43, 57-59, and 76-79. Even more explicit is Ellul's remark in his article "Karl Barth and Us," Sojourners (December 1978): 24, in which he mentions "the error so often made in the U.S. of considering me a 'Calvinist.'" In her dissertation, p. 159, footnote #90, Temple recalls that Ellul made this same point to her in a personal interview.

9

2. Ellul and Barth

Another slant on the idea that Ellul's methodology is that of a "theological positivist" pertains to the influence which Karl Barth has exercised on him. Both Cobb and Pannenberg, for example, use Barth as a prime example of theological positivism.[53] If the evidence for Ellul's "Calvinism" is, at best, tenuous, there is much truth in saying that Ellul follows in the theological footsteps of Barth.

Ellul's discovery of Barth completely effaced the influence of Calvin: "Obviously, once I began reading Karl Barth, I stopped being a Calvinist."[54] In several places and in many ways Ellul affirms the deep and distant roots of his thought which are "nourished in the ever fertile soil of Soren Kierkegaard and Karl Barth."[55] In several places he expresses amazement at those who suggest that Barth's theology is antiquated or obsolete. In his mind, "Barth endures...as a continual resource for continual theological research."[56] This direct influence on his theology is seen in a variety of instances, including Ellul's thoughts on prayer,[57] the interplay of divine and human freedom,[58] the universal salvation of all

---

[53]See footnotes #24 and #28 above. Gordon Kaufman castigates such positivism as "the fundamental error of the most powerful theological construction of this century, that of Karl Barth." See his An Essay on Theological Method (Missoula, M.T.: Scholars Press, 1975), p. 68, footnote #23. Compare his similar comments on page 57.

[54]Jacques Ellul, Perspectives on Our Age (New York: Seabury, 1981), p. 17. Hereafter cited as POOA. Jean-Marc Berthoud is one of the few interpreters who have recognized this shift in Ellul's thought. See his article, "Jacques Ellul et l'impossible dialectique entre Marx et Calvin," La Revue Réformée 33, no. 4 (1982): 181.

[55]Idem, Living Faith, p. ix.

[56]Idem, "Karl Barth and Us," p. 22. See also POOA, p. 18.

[57]Idem, Ethics of Freedom, pp. 126-127. Note, however, Ellul's short caveat on Barth's doctrine of prayer in his book Prayer and Modern Man, trans. Edward Hopkin (New York: Seabury, 1970), pp. 47-50.

[58]This is best seen in Ellul's book The Politics of God and the Politics of Man, trans. Geoffrey Bromiley (Grand Rapids: Eerdmans, 1972), the entire theme of which is this interplay.

people,[59] scripture,[60] his contrasting of religion and revelation,[61] his Christocentricity,[62] and his affirmation of the importance of human initiative and works.[63]

Despite these many and significant similarities, however, Ellul explicitly repudiates the charge that he is anything like an unconditional Barthian. That, he observes, would betray the very spirit of Barth. Thus, it is misleading to describe Ellul simply as "a disciple of Barth,"[64] or his theology as "almost wholly Barthian"[65] and "uncompromisingly Barthian."[66]

More judicious are the works by Fasching, Gill, Bromiley and Vahanian, all of whom acknowledge Ellul's similarities to Barth but also recognize his peculiar diversions and departures from Barth. Fasching sees Barth as Ellul's point of departure, but is quick to point out that he in no way slavishly follows

---

[59]Ellul, "Karl Barth and Us," p. 24. A distinction should be made, however, for if Barth's universalism is somewhat latent, as some suggest, Ellul's, on the other hand, is explicit and wholehearted. See footnote #44 above for references to Ellul's doctrine of universalism.

[60]Ibid., pp. 22-23. See ISOS, p. 78.

[61]Idem, Living Faith pp. 125-126, and POOA, p. 93.

[62]Geoffrey Bromiley, "Barth's Influence on Jacques Ellul," in JE:IE, pp. 32-51.

[63]According to Ellul, Barth "puts mankind back into theology," (ISOS, p. 79).

[64]Burke, p. 17.

[65]L. Richard Bradley, "The Kingdom of God and Social Change in the Thought of Jacques Ellul" (ThM thesis, Princeton Theological Seminary, 1971), p. 32. Note Bradley's comparison of Barth and Ellul on pages 27-34 of his thesis.

[66]Stephen Rose, "Whither Ethics, Jacques Ellul?" p. 124. Ellul rejects this charge in his article "Karl Barth and Us," p. 22, and in The Ethics of Freedom, p. 8.

the Swiss master.[67] Vahanian shows how Ellul will readily embrace positions which are diametrically opposed to Barth.[68] Gill, who is probably the most perceptive of current Ellul interpreters, has a ready eye for the continuity and divergence between the two thinkers. While acknowledging the above-mentioned similarities, he also notes a host of divergences, such as Ellul's more explicit affirmation of universalism, his peculiar interpretation of the Apostle Paul's use of the word exousia, his even greater emphasis on God as Wholly Other, and Barth's more affirmative and positive ideas on the role of the state. According to Gill, despite his clear debt to Barth, Ellul's debt to Kierkegaard is even more profound.[69]

We briefly mention even more differences. Ellul rejects the just war theory.[70] He criticizes Barth's statements on work, the death penalty, and vocation as anachronistic, abstract, and idealistic.[71] Ellul wants to go beyond Barth by formulating a viable Christian ethic, a task he feels is made difficult by the inherent tendency of Barthian theology to

---

[67]Darrell Fasching, "The Apocalypse of Freedom: Christian Ethics in the Technological Society. A Defense of the Social Ethics of Jacques Ellul," 2 vols. (PhD dissertation, Syracuse University, 1978), pp. 21-24. Fasching makes the same point in his book, The Thought of Jacques Ellul, pp. 6-8. His book is a revision of his dissertation, and only half as long as the latter. In personal correspondence, however, Fasching wrote to me that he felt his book was a substantial improvement and that it left out nothing of strategic importance that was in his dissertation (Darrell Fasching to Dan Clendenin, August 10, 1984).

[68]Vahanian, "Jacques Ellul and the Religious Illusion," p. xviii.

[69]David Gill, The Word of God in the Ethics of Jacques Ellul (Metuchen, NJ: Scarecrow Press, 1984), pp. 163, 47, 159, 109, 160-161, and 179. This book is an updated version of Gill's doctoral dissertation, with very few changes, entitled "The Word of God in the Ethics of Jacques Ellul" (PhD dissertation, University of Southern California, 1979).

[70]Jacques Ellul, Violence: Reflections from a Christian Perspective, trans. Cecelia Gaul Kings (New York: Seabury, 1969), pp. 4-7.

[71]Idem, The Ethics of Freedom, pp. 456-461.

become other-wordly with its stress on transcendence.[72] Finally, we mention Ellul's repugnance towards Barth's rigid systematizing.[73] With typically judicious wisdom, Bromiley writes that there is a "close relation between Ellul and Barth; nevertheless, they must be set in perspective...In some areas Barth influenced him greatly, but in many others he did not."[74]

To conclude this section, we can affirm, then, that while Ellul might be described as a "theological positivist," care must be taken to explain what this means.[75] While Calvin influenced Ellul at one point in his theological development, it is inaccurate to label him a "Calvinist," for in many ways and for a long time now he has parted company with the French Reformer. His affinities to Barth are more numerous, but even here it is facile to overlook Ellul's readiness to dispatch Barth for his own ideas. Still others, though, would prefer to read Ellul not as a theological positivist, but as an existentialist. This reading is our next consideration.

C. Ellul as Existentialist

Other people classify Ellul's primary methodological emphasis as existentialist. Without attempting to sort through the multitude of definitions for "existentialist," a word whose definition, Cobb notes, "remains as confusing as ever,"[76] we can simplify our task by following the lead of Alasdair MacIntyre. MacIntyre specifies a handful of recurring themes in "existentialism." Then, we can observe how closely Ellul typifies such a schema, and the extent to which the secondary

---

[72] Idem, False Presence of the Kingdom, trans. C. Edward Hopkin (New York: Seabury, 1972), p. 7. Hereafter referred to as FPOK. Compare Ellul's similar comments in ISOS, p. 175.

[73] Idem, The Ethics of Freedom, p. 158.

[74] Bromiley, pp. 33-34.

[75] Egbert Schuurman, for example, uses the term "positivist" in a different way in his description of various attitudes toward technology. According to Schuurman, Ellul is not a "positivist" but a "transcendentalist." See his book Technology and the Future: A Philosophical Challenge, trans. Herbert Donald Morton (Toronto: Wedge Publishing Foundation, 1980), pp. 51-52, and 125-158.

[76] Cobb, p. 200. Cobb attempts to define the word both historically and as an ideal type (pp. 199-226).

literature on him picks this up. According to MacIntyre, "existentialism" involves six key themes: the individual versus the system or the mass, intentionality, being and absurdity, the nature and significance of choice, the role of extreme experiences, and the nature of communication.[77] With this non-technical working definition in mind, we can now examine the extent to which Ellul can be read as an existentialist.

Ellul's thought exhibits nearly all of these themes mentioned by MacIntyre, and in this sense he might well be called an existentialist, but not with the sense of adhering to any systematic philosophy or school of thought by that name.[78] Ellul's primary concern is concrete, real-life existence. He disdains the purely abstract, the questions of "essence," and in his personal life he is anything but an ivory-towered scholar. "We are touching on a trait I consider important: I never write ideas. I have always attempted to transmit exactly what I have experienced...I always write about my experience."[79] Several examples show how Ellul's thought flows out of his personal experience, and how, to use Tillich's distinction, Ellul attempts to avoid the detached objectivity of the philosopher in favor of existential involvement in the common lot of all people.[80]

His attraction to Marx is partly explained by his family's poverty.[81] His frustrations with the bureaucratized and institutionalized church come from his 21 years on the National Council of the Reformed Church of France.[82] One must also be aware of his significant political involvement to appreciate his criticism of that realm. During the 1930's this included the

---

[77]The Encyclopedia of Philosophy, 1972 reprint edition, s.v. "Existentialism," by Alasdair MacIntyre.

[78]Vernard Eller, "Ellul and Kierkegaard: Closer than Brothers," in JE:IE, p. 57. Like Gill, Eller suggests that Ellul is more akin to Kierkegaard than to Barth.

[79]Ellul, ISOS, pp. 67, 189.

[80]Paul Tillich, Systematic Theology, volume 1 (Chicago: University of Chicago Press, 1951), pp. 22-23.

[81]Ellul, ISOS, p. 11, and 217. See also POOA, pages 1-5. In addition, we might mention that his rejection of Marx was partly due to Marx's inability to address what Ellul calls the "existential questions" of life, death and love (POOA, p. 14).

[82]See the entire chapter 6 of ISOS, where Ellul writes of his many church involvements.

Popular Front and the Personalist Movement. During the 1940's he was a leader in the French Resistance and then served on the mayoral staff of Bordeaux after the war. He was keenly interested in and closely linked with the ferment about the Spanish and Algerian revolutions. Yet all of this "formed an accumulation of ruined revolutionary possibilities. After this, I never believed anything could be changed by this route [of politics]."[83]

Another common theme in Ellul's work, the first of the six listed by MacIntyre, is his stress on the individual. Indeed, his whole problem with the "technological society" is not that technique per se is bad, but what Menninger aptly describes as society's "suppressive homogeneity" and "the loss by man of his responsibility to himself and others."[84] Only a recovery of the responsible individual is sufficient to reorient one towards integrity and authentic existence. Many, in fact, criticize Ellul harshly for what they perceive as his radical subjectivity, yet he continues to insist that the situation warrants the stress: "our hope lies in starting from the individual--from total subjectivity."[85] The West's only hope for survival, he maintains, requires us "to start at the most profound human level; the collective project can only be stirred by a new thrust of the individual...the individual's will to reassert himself in the etymological sense of the word (individuus: the central kernel that cannot be divided)."[86] His proposed "ethics of freedom," then, "can be demonstrated only by individual acts in individual people."[87]

---

[83] Idem, ISOS, p. 56.

[84] David C. Menninger, "Technique and Politics: The Political Thought of Jacques Ellul" (PhD dissertation, University of California, Riverside, 1974), pp. 182, 163.

[85] Jacques Ellul, "Between Chaos and Paralysis," The Christian Century 85 (June 5, 1968): 749.

[86] Idem, "Search for an Image," The Humanist (November-December, 1973): 25.

[87] Idem, The Ethics of Freedom, p. 210. See Ellul's similar emphases in his book The Judgement of Jonah, trans. Geoffrey Bromiley (Grand Rapids: Eerdmans, 1971), p. 22. Temple acknowledges the validity of criticizing Ellul for excessive individualism, but in her discussion of Ellul's doctrine of the church (pp. 13-48), she tempers the charge by showing Ellul's stress on community. See pages 29-30, in particular, of her dissertation.

Intentionality, choice and human initiative constitute MacIntyre's second and fourth characteristics, and these too find an important place in Ellul's thought. The recovery of freedom by individual persons who exercise authentic human initiative comprises the sum and substance of the Christian life, according to Ellul. People must exercise this initiative because fate begins to operate when they give up. The "extreme experiences" or what MacIntyre calls the focus on absurdity (his third and fifth specifications) of modern society make human initiative all the more urgent. Ellul's marked apocalypticism is well known. According to his sociological analyses, ours is an age of unprecedented complexity, insecurity and anxiety. This theme runs throughout Ellul's work, from his earliest to his more recent writings.[88] Life itself, he suggests, has become absurd, a well-worn aphorism, to be sure, but not for that reason any less true.

Jesus Christ alone, the absolute paradox to use Kierkegaard's term, provides individuals with their only hope for combating these dreadful experiences of "insoluble anguish."[89] Having chosen to follow Him, we enter into a Christian life of radical discipleship. Prayer, for example, requires of us "a radical trust, to the point of the absurd...What is required of us is a blind act of faith...[an] irrational decision."[90] The Christian lives in solitude and in suffering, rejecting the "Christian security in a Christianized society"[91] where the faith has been reduced to "a handful of axioms."[92] This often

---

[88]See, for example, his The Presence of the Kingdom, trans. Olive Wyon (Philadelphia: Westminster Press, 1951), pp. 31-32; and Living Faith, pages 201ff., where Ellul laments the "rising tide of disaster." I disagree at this point with Temple, who writes that Ellul "does not say that our civilization is any worse than previous ones" (p. 178). Ellul's whole sociological analysis seems intent on showing that our modern situation is fundamentally different from those in the past, in the worst sense, not only in degree but in kind.

[89]Ellul, The Ethics of Freedom, p. 45.

[90]Idem, Prayer and Modern Man, trans. C. Edward Hopkin (New York: Seabury, 1979) pp. 141-142. For other examples of the "absurdity" of Jesus Christ and the Christian life, see The Politics of God and the Politics of Man, pp. 30, 36, 75, and The Judgement of Jonah, pp. 26-27.

[91]Ibid., p. 63.

[92]Idem, The Ethics of Freedom, p. 100.

requires a "teleological suspension of the ethical" good in favor of doing God's will.[93] Indeed, to pick up on another of MacIntyre's categories, his sixth, the very nature of Ellul's communication is also quite "existential," with his stated purpose being to provoke his readers to responsible decisions and critical self-awareness. Ellul continually refuses to provide his audience with readymade "solutions" to the problems which he describes. His books have another purpose, "to provoke a reaction of personal reflection, and thus to obligate the reader to choose for himself a course of action...The real question is to know if one can act as a responsible man on his own."[94]

If all this sounds explicitly Kierkegaardian, there is a good reason. Ellul acknowledges his debt to "the father of existentialism," a fact which we have already noted above.[95] Kierkegaard, he writes, more than any other Christian writer, "is the one who has given us the best, the most genuine, the most radical account of the existential reality of faith."[96] This debt is most apparent in one of his most recent books La Subversion du christianisme. In a review of the book in Fides et Historia David Gill draws out several parallels.[97] Ellul's theological and biblical studies bear out this Kierkegaardian connection with their many references to him. It is no wonder, then, that many of his interpreters read Ellul primarily as an

---

[93] Ellul explicitly affirms this Kierkegaardian concept. See To Will and to Do, pp. 206-208, Violence, pp. 160-162, and The Politics of God and the Politics of Man, p. 105.

[94] Ellul, "Interviews with Jacques Ellul, October 20, 24, and 30, 1973, Bordeaux, France," in Menninger's dissertation, p. 217. The emphasis is his. See Ellul's similar comment in The Technological Society, trans. John Wilkinson (New York: Knopf, 1964), p. xxxiii.

[95] See footnote #55 above, and also ISOS, pp. 17, 59, and 81.

[96] Ellul, Living Faith, p. 106.

[97] According to Gill, Ellul restates for the 20th century the problem which Kierkegaard raised for the previous century: "Why is Christendom so little like Biblical Christianity?" He goes on to suggest that the parallels between Kierkegaard and Ellul are "very explicit." See his book review of Ellul's Subversion in Fides et Historia, Volume XVII, No. 2 (Spring-Summer 1985): 70-77.

existentialist. Christians,[98] Outka,[99] Sullivan and DiMaio,[100] Gill,[101] Burke,[102] and others all recognize these roots. The most insistent advocate of this reading of Ellul is the Kierkegaardian scholar Vernard Eller. In his several articles on Ellul he confirms the impression that Ellul is indeed an "existentialist" in the general sense of the term, with particular roots in Kierkegaard: "Ellul is an existential thinker, and what that signifies is not any particular connection with the school of philosophy known as 'existentialism' but a driving concern to be practical, down to earth, edifying, dealing with the actual situations in which men find themselves."[103] Like Gill above, Eller contends that it is Kierkegaard the existentialist, not Barth the positivist, "for whom Ellul shows the most sympathy."[104] As we have already observed, Ellul displays an almost cavalier attitude toward abstract theologizing, which, he writes "bores me immeasurably...All these treatises on the nature of God do not interest me in the least. What is important to me is that which belongs to the ethical

---

[98]Clifford G. Christians, "Ellul on Solution: An Alternative but no Prophecy," in JE:IE, p. 160.

[99]Outka, pp. 195-196, 212.

[100]Robert R. Sullivan and Alfred J. DiMaio, "Jacques Ellul: Toward Understanding His Political Thinking," Journal of Church and State, vol. 24, no. 1 (Winter 1982):17-18, 21-22. The authors note "the primal Kierkegaardian quality" of some of Ellul's books.

[101]Gill, The Word of God in the Ethics of Jacques Ellul, pp. 31, 163.

[102]Burke, p. 249.

[103]Vernard Eller, "Jacques Ellul, The Polymath Who Knows Only One Thing," Brethren Life and Thought 18 (Winter 1973): 79. See Eller's other article, "Four Who Remember: Kierkegaard, the Blumhardts, Ellul, and Muggeridge," Katallagete: Be Reconciled 3, no. 3 (Spring 1971): 6-12. See footnote #78 above.

[104]Eller, "Ellul and Kierkegaard: Closer than Brothers," p. 52. See Gill's The Word of God in the Ethics of Jacques Ellul, p. 163. We should note that these two methodological perspectives of "positivist" and "existentialist" are by no means necessarily exclusive of each other. Kierkegaard belongs to both categories, as Cobb points out (Living Options in Protestant Theology, A Survey of Methods, p. 200).

18

domain and the existential domain, in other words, what is   close
to life, to reality."[105]

D. Ellul as Prophet

We come now to the somewhat unconventional designation of
Ellul's theological method as "prophetic."   Several factors,
however, warrant the use of this nomenclature.   First, in book
after book Ellul has written extensively on what he describes as
the "unique prophetic calling of Christians."[106]   We must,
then, explore what Ellul means by this and his own selfunder-
standing as a Christian who attempts to fulfill this calling.

Secondly, an overwhelming number of people have referred to
Ellul as a "prophet."   Temple, for example, refers to Ellul's
prophetic modus operandi.[107] Hanks writes that "when reading
the reviews--from very diverse sources--of [Ellul's] books, the
adjective 'prophetic' appears so frequently that it almost
becomes a refrain."[108]   This "prophetic" description often
carries with it a pejorative sense, especially for those who see
Ellul as a "theologian of gloom,"[109] or a "utopian."[110] We
shall illustrate the charge of prophetic pessimism below.

Third, although the "prophetic methodology" is hardly a
commonplace, we need not feel compelled to think in only
traditional categories. Other scholars in different fields have
used the prophetic model with creative results. Two examples
illustrate this. Edward Ross addressed the American Sociological
Society on the subject of "The Sociologist in the Role of the

---

[105]Ellul, ISOS, p. 220. Temple, therefore, suggests that
Ellul is a sort of "phenomenologist," that is, one interested in
real life phenomena. See her dissertation, p. 75.

[106]Idem, Autopsy of Revolution, trans. Patricia Wolf (New
York: Knopf, 1971), p. 231. Hereafter referred to as Autopsy.

[107]Temple, pp. 36-46.

[108]Hanks, "Jacques Ellul: The Original Liberation
Theologian," p. 11.

[109]Charles Dollen, Best Sellers 1 (July 1, 1973): 162.

[110]Fasching's basic criticism of Ellul is that he is a
"utopian" who prescribes a "more with less" ethical theory.

Prophet."[111]   More   recently, in the realm of political science,
Neal Riemer has argued that, when properly understood, "Prophetic
Politics"   serve   as   a   more   promising   model   for   politics.[112]
Ellul the polymath fits well into both   roles   as   a   sociologist
and   a political scientist, and hence we do well to take the lead
of Ross and Riemer   and   apply   the   "prophetic"   designation   to
Ellul's   theological   methodology.   If William Gorman is correct,
a right reading of Ellul is not   only   enhanced   by   but   depends
upon   "the   realization   that   this   [Ellul's   work] is prophesy"
(sic).[113]

Most of the thinkers   just   cited   use   the   word   "prophet"
without   ever   defining   it.   My purpose here is not to classify
all of the various   definitions   or   nuances   of   the   word,   but
simply   to   show   that this is a category which writers are using
to describe Ellul.   For our own definition of the word, as it   is
used   to   describe   Ellul,   Gill's   article   by   this title is an
excellent start.[114]

According to Gill, by definition, a prophet   expounds   God's
word   to   His   people, making special appeals to their particular
circumstances.   A prophet provokes us and attempts   to   shake   us
out of our rituals, our comfortable status quo.   Both the content
and the style go together to help define the prophet.   Following

---

[111]Edward A. Ross, "The   Sociologist   in   the   Role   of   the
Prophet,"   American Sociological Review 8 (February 1943): 10-14.
Despite the possibilities of abuse, Ross contends that "there   is
still   a   place   for the modest and wary forecaster" (p. 14).   As
can be seen from this quote, Ross's primary emphasis was   on   the
sociologist's   ability   to predict future trends, based on scientific   research.   Ellul   writes   that   Christians   should   serve
society in this capacity.

[112]Neal   Riemer,   "The   Future of the Democratic Revolution:
Toward a more Prophetic Politics," Humanities   in   Society   (Fall
1983):   5-18.   Riemer's   "four major commitments" of a prophetic
politics are unusually close to some   of   Ellul's   own   concerns.
These   include   what   Riemer calls "values of a superior order...
fearless   criticism   of   existing   political   orders...creative
constitutional   breakthroughs...and   futuristic   projection   via
imaginative scenarios" (p. 9).

[113]William   Gorman,   "Jacques   Ellul: A   Prophetic   Voice,"
Center Magazine 1 (October-November 1967): 34.

[114]David   Gill,   "Jacques Ellul: The Prophet as Theologian,"
Themelios (September 1981): 4-14.

Gill's own procedure,[115] we can best define this word by letting Ellul speak for himself. Thus our own definition of a prophet will attempt to approximate his.

What, according to Ellul, does the prophetic role of a Christian entail, given his suggestion that "every Christian who has received the Holy Spirit is now a prophet"?[116] In general, we can say that it requires the reintroduction of meaningful revolution into society. In Ellul's judgment, true revolution is dead and gone (thus his Autopsy). Nothing is more needed and less certain than the possibility of social revolution in the constructive sense. Christians, however, introduce a prophetic presence of the future kingdom into the world today, and by so doing constitute "an inexhaustible revolutionary force in the midst of the world."[117]

In particular, the Christian's prophetic vocation requires of him or her a host of revolutionary duties. He is an advocate of the disenfranchised.[118] He desacralizes and demythologizes the sacred commonplaces of society through a rejection of all forms of idealism and the adoption of a concrete realism which ruthlessly criticizes all things.[119] Above all, the prophetic ministry of the church serves the world as a sentinel or a "watchman." That is, the Christian warns, alerts, and provokes society, even as Jonah did to Nineveh and Ezekiel to Israel.[120]

---

[115]Gill quotes The Politics of God and the Politics of Man (pp. 20-21, 47, and 50) for Ellul's own definition of a prophet.

[116]Ellul, POK, p. 50.

[117]Ibid., p. 42. Compare this entire chapter II on "Revolutionary Christianity."

[118]Idem, Violence, p. 155.

[119]Idem, Hope in Time of Abandonment, trans. C. Edward Hopkin (New York: Seabury, 1973), pp. 274-282. Hereafter referred to as Hope. I have intentionally used the language of Marx here. Several scholars have pointed out how Ellul reverses the program of Bultmann. The latter intends to demythologize the Bible, while the former wants to demythologize modern society.

[120]Idem, The Theological Foundation of Law, trans. Marguerite Wieser (New York: Seabury, 1969), p. 134. See FPOK, pp. 186-190, and his article "Mirror of These Ten Years," page 45, where Ellul discusses this subject.

Ellul, then, has no choice but to see himself as a "prophet" of sorts. Gill, who more than any other Ellul interpreter promotes this designation of Ellul, suggests that Ellul would resist the designation and would be embarrassed by it, but this cannot be the case. Ellul even refers to the special function of scholars vis-à-vis the prophetic calling of Christians, in distinction from non-intellectuals.[121] In one of his recent books he describes his own vocation as follows: "[T]he only thing left is the prophet's cry...I cry out because I see the end...and all my books, cold as they are, must be heard as cries."[122]

Many of his interpreters have picked up on such passages as the one just quoted and concluded the Ellul the prophet is no more than a disenchanted naysayer. Manfred Stanley, for example, mentions Ellul as among those who espouse their "pessimist prophecy."[123] Rupert Hall labels Ellul as a "prophet whose cry is only 'Woe, ye are damned...' [and who] looks forward with only despair, disgust and rage."[124] Ellul is well aware of this charge and has responded to it. He makes several points worth noting.

First, technique per se is not evil ("an absurd notion which I have never suggested"); the problem is "the present structure of society."[125] That is, technique now defines our

---

[121]Idem, Apocalypse, p. 127. See also Ellul's chapter IV in POK which treats of this matter.

[122]Idem, Living Faith, p. 201.

[123]Manfred Stanley, The Technological Conscience: Survival and Dignity in an Age of Expertise (New York: Free Press, 1978), p. 45.

[124]A. Rupert Hall, "An Unconvincing Indictment of the Evils of Technology," Scientific American 212 (February 1965): 126, 128. The emphasis is his own. This quote is telling, for it betrays Hall's total ignorance of Ellul's unbounded optimism based on his belief in the universal salvation of all people. For other references to Ellul as a prophet, see the dissertations by Fasching (pp. 10, 12-20) and Duane Miller, "The Effect of Technology upon Humanization in the Thought of Lewis Mumford and Jacques Ellul" (PhD dissertation, Boston University, 1970), pp. 23-33. Ihara devoted a section of his dissertation to Ellul as a prophet (pp. 21-31).

[125]Ellul, Autopsy, p. 275.

very environment and comprises a virtually impenetrable "system" (to use the word from his book The Technological System). Merely to focus on the disagreeable aspects of technology, though, creates what Ellul calls a false problem. Second, Ellul advocates "not an antitechnicism or a judgement against technology" but its "critical acceptance."[126]   Third, Ellul has never denied that technology has brought elements of well-being and happiness to modern man. He simply has not discussed these, he says, because they are so obvious.[127]   In fact he even says that he is convinced that "the possibilities of human survival are better served by more technique than less."[128]   Fourth, due to Ellul's theological convictions about the universal salvation of all people beyond history, he even goes so far as to describe himself as "utterly optimistic."[129]

Apart from those who have neither the time nor the inclination to accept Ellul at his word and to appreciate the nuance of his arguments, there is another group of interpreters who are more judicious in their understanding of Ellul as a prophet. Chief among these is David Gill, whom we shall use as an example.

Gill, like Gorman, is convinced that Ellul is best understood not as a teacher whose chief concern is rigorous systematizing or order, but as a prophet whose goal is to provoke, reorient and motivate us by mediating the word of the Wholly Other God to the contemporary situation.[130]   Both the content and style (hyperbole, overstatement, generalizations, and absolutistic rhetoric) lead Gill to this conclusion. Ellul's

---

[126]Idem, POOA, p. 108.

[127]Idem, "The Biology of Technique," The Nation CC (May 24, 1965): 568.

[128]Idem, "The Technological Order," in Carl Mitcham and Robert Mackey, eds., Philosophy and Technology, Readings in the Philosophical Problems of Technology (New York: The Free Press, 1972), p. 86. As one example of this, we can note Ellul's proposal for a new socialism of decentralized decision making which is made possible by micro-computers. See his article, "Pour un socialisme tout autre," Réforme 1977 (March 12, 1983): 7. Cf. Joyce Hanks, p. 89.

[129]Idem, ISOS, p. 82. Compare his response to the charge of excessive pessimism in The Technological Society, pages xvii-xxxiii.

[130]David Gill, "Jacques Ellul: The Prophet as Theologian."

prophetic significance, then, "lies not only in challenging our intellectual constructs, or dogmatics, but in pressing toward the concrete meaning of faith for life in this area."[131] Although he concludes that Ellul's work "can stand on its own as sociological or theological criticism and construction," we risk misinterpreting him if we demand that he conform to the normal canons of logic.[132]

E. Ellul as Dialectician

A final way to understand Ellul's project is to appreciate his devotion to a dialectical method, one of the most quoted and least understood aspects of his work. This will be the perspective which we will adopt in the ensuing chapters of this work. Temple writes that "the decisive and yet most elusive problem...is the recognition of the centrality of dialectics in every part of Ellul's outlook."[133] As this will be the subject of an extended treatment in the next chapter, our comments here, and especially our analysis of Ellul's use and definition of dialectic, will be limited.

There is no doubt that Ellul is fiercely devoted to a dialectical method: "I am a dialectician above all; I believe nothing can be understood without dialectical analysis."[134] He laments the general neglect and rejection of this method in favor of a purely linear logic. This uncompromising devotion to dialectics almost always acts as a stumbling block for many of his readers, as Walters-Bugbee shows,[135] while for others it

---

[131]Ibid., p. 13.

[132]Idem, The Word of God in the Ethics of Jacques Ellul, p. 183. This precise point becomes a problem for some. Does Ellul's "prophetic methodology" excuse his repeated overstatements, generalizations, and occasional tortured logic, or are we justified in forcing him to adhere to the canons of logic? See Arthur Holmes, "On Pushing a Prophet," Reformed Journal 32 (November 1982): 8. Holmes also has an article on Ellul in JE:IE, entitled "Ellul on Natural Law" (pp. 241-245), in which he makes some of these same criticisms.

[133]Temple, p. 5. Compare her definitions of this on p. 99 of her dissertation.

[134]Ellul, "Interviews," p. 224.

[135]Walters-Bugbee, ibid. Compare Wren's dissertation, p. 2.

represents Ellul's genius. As Burke correctly notes, "Ellul's entire analysis will appeal primarily to those individuals who see dialectical theology as a useful enterprise."[136] Hollenbach, to cite a contrary example, criticizes Ellul for rejecting "coherent persuasion for the mode of prophetic denunciation," and suggests that Ellul's theological method "represents dialectical theology run amuck."[137] Those who do not appreciate or understand Ellul's commitment to a dialectical method will not go far in interpreting his project.

One example of misinterpreting Ellul on this basis is the nearly ubiquitous charge that he is a fatalist and a pessimist. According to Ellul, it is often the failure to understand his dialectical method which produces the misinterpretation: "You can easily see that I am wrongly called a pessimist. Pessimism is not the word; it is rather a negativity within a dialectical process."[138] As in Hegel, there is for Ellul a positive aspect even in the negative pole of the dialectic. For Ellul, technique serves as the negative pole of a dialectic which, overall, has a positive outcome.

Marx, on the social scientific level, and Barth, on the theological level, combine to form the roots of Ellul's dialectical method. Ellul read Marx's Das Kapital when he was nineteen, and was immediately convinced by it: "It answered almost all the questions I had been asking myself...It seemed to me that the method of Karl Marx...was superior to all that I had encountered elsewhere."[139] Marx, however, could not answer some of Ellul's existential concerns, and he subsequently underwent what he calls a violent and brutal conversion to Christianity. From this "double conversion" to Marx and the Bible there emerged the beginning point of Ellul's dialectical method:

> I thus remained unable to eliminate Marx, unable to eliminate the biblical revelation, and unable to merge the two. For me, it was impossible to put them together. So I began to be torn between the two, and I have remained so all my life. The development of

---

[136] Burke, p. 255.

[137] David Hollenbach, review of The Ethics of Freedom, in Theological Studies vol. 37, no. 4 (December 1976): 710.

[138] Ellul, ISOS, p. 208.

[139] Idem, "From Jacques Ellul," in Introducing Jacques Ellul, p.5.

my thinking can be explained starting with this distinction.[140]

Elsewhere Ellul refers to this as "my own twofold intellectual origin in Marx and Barth [in which] dialectic has a central place for me."[141]

There is no doubt that the "dialectical" method is hard to understand, for different people use the term in different ways. American readers, especially, Ellul suggests, find the method hard to understand. All the more reason, then, for our Chapter Two in which we will explore this in depth. According to Ellul, "[T]here is a dialectic within my work, and it is entirely central in that I have discovered progressively that in the world we live in there are no means of thinking and acquiring knowledge that are not of a dialectical nature...I became conscious, as I worked and thought, that I needed to interpret all things in a dialectical manner."[142] Because nearly all of his interpreters recognize this dialectical nature of Ellul's thought, which is not to say that they understand it fully, we will save our further discussion of it, and the secondary literature, for the ensuing chapter.

F. Conclusion

We may end this overview of Ellul's interpreters with several observations about the status of Ellul research. First, for the first time researchers now have immediate access to a near-exhaustive bibliography on Ellul, including both primary

---

[140]Idem, ISOS, p. 16.

[141]Idem, "On Dialectic," in JE:IE, p. 292. On Barth's influence in this respect, see POOA (pp. 17-18). On Kierkegaard's similar influence, see Eller's article in Christians and Van Hook (pp. 54-56). Berthoud refers to the dialectic between Marx and Calvin/Barth as "impossible." His article which we cited above offers a stinging, if superficial, critique of Ellul's dialectic. According to Berthoud, Ellul's dialectic unjustifiably separates the phenomenal/existential (cf. Marx) and the noumenal/theological (cf. Barth). This opposition, writes Berthoud, "is characteristic of all the thought stemming from the Kantian neo-orthodoxy of Barth" (p. 184). He suggests that Ellul's prodigious talent is a wealth wasted and ruined: "Dieu veuille qu'il revienne de cette voie de perdition!" (p. 188).

[142]Idem, ISOS, pp. 201-202.

and secondary literature. Hank's Jacques Ellul: A Comprehensive Bibliography succeeded in exploding at least one mistaken notion about Ellul, the idea that little had been written on him. Just the opposite is true, and while this may complicate research in some ways, a more accurate picture of Ellul is possible than ever before. Hanks is already at work on a supplement to her bibliography which is due out in March, 1987.[143]

Secondly, no excuse remains for misunderstanding Ellul's definition and exposition of what he calls "technique." There have been numerous rehearsals, for example, of his characterology of technique as found in his two works devoted to the subject, all of which show quite well what Ellul is about.[144] He is not an anti-technist. Technique goes far beyond mere machines or computers. We need not rehearse these points. Little mention, in fact, will be made of technique in this work, for the secondary literature has done more than enough on it to make clear Ellul's position.

Third, more biographical information on Ellul is now available than ever before. These include his Perspectives On Our Age (1981) and In Season, Out of Season (1982). Researchers should also be aware that Ellul has already written a two-volume autobiography which will be published only after his death (due to his hatred of sensationalism and exhibitionism).[145] Special mention should be made of Gary Wren's dissertation in this regard. In his first chapter Wren does an excellent job of outlining the social and historical background of the France (1900-1954) in which Ellul grew up. Although some of his conclusions are reductionistic and simplistic (for example, that Ellul's project is mainly a reaction against "those socio-economic developments which eventually destroyed the social and moral order of his early formative years"[146]), he nevertheless has provided readers with the only overview available on Ellul's Sitz im Leben. At any rate, the biographical and autobiographical advances should help to prevent further misinterpretations of Ellul, such as that he is a Calvinist, a charge he explicitly denies in In Season, Out of Season.

---

[143]Joyce Hanks to Dan Clendenin, June 21, 1986.

[144]See Temple, for an example of this, pages 435-443, and the section entitled "Technique is not the Enemy."

[145]Hanks, "Jacques Ellul: The Original Liberation Theologian," p. 11, footnote #44.

[146]Wren, p. 49.

Fourth, and most importantly, the secondary literature bears out the conclusion that Ellul is a generalist with wide interests, and that his method is what we might call "eclectic." Any understanding of Ellul depends upon this important point. Wren, for example, is no doubt correct to write about the "wild eclecticism" of Ellul's sociological theory.[147] Likewise, Temple points out that his sociological methods do not fit into standard categories.[148] Those who variously interpret Ellul as a positivist, existentialist, prophet and dialectician all have good reasons for doing so. Ellul is all of these, and yet not any one of them exclusively. His approach is multifaceted, and this, in part, explains both his broad appeal to social scientists, theologians of the left and right, biblical scholars, and political scientists, and the criticism from these same quarters. One can correctly argue, I think, that this multifaceted character of his method represents both a strength and a weakness in Ellul. He wants to see the big picture from several intellectual vantage points. He bemoans our age of specialization in minutiae. By doing so he courts the wrath of those specialists. In this eclectic approach the whole is bigger than any of its constituent parts.[149]

---

[147] Ibid., p. 146.

[148] Temple, p. 168.

[149] Temple, pp. 4-5. Temple rightly observes that Ellul's works comprise a coherent whole which avoids the pitfalls of systematization and fragmentation.

CHAPTER TWO

ELLUL'S DIALECTICAL METHOD

It is of the highest importance to ascertain and understand
rightly the nature of Dialectic. Wherever there is movement, wherever there is life, wherever anything is carried
into effect in the actual world, there Dialectic is at
work. It is also the soul of all knowledge which is truly
scientific.[1]

A. Introduction

Despite Ellul's essential divergence from Hegel's idea of
dialectic, and the anachronistic relationship of the quote to
Ellul, the latter's advice is timely in any attempt to
understand the former's intellectual method. If Ellul is a
theological positivist, existentialist or prophet, he is, even
more so, a dialectician. In fact, we could subsume the first
three categories under the fourth. Thus, dialectic is, to use
Hegel's words on the subject, the heart and soul of all
knowledge. This is certainly true in regards to Ellul's
method. That is, dialectic is the kernel, the operative
assumption which underlies all he has written. Those for whom
dialectic is a stumbling block or a rock of offence will never
appreciate or understand Ellul. While the strategic importance
of dialectic for Ellul has been amply noted by many, only one
article exists on the matter (by John Boli-Bennett). This
chapter attempts to fill this important void. From the last
chapter on the general idea of Ellul as an "eclectic," we now
move to the more particular idea of his specifically dialectical
method.

The course of this chapter is as follows. After a background section in which we establish what, exactly, "dialectic"
is, both in general and in particular as used by theology, we
shall examine Ellul's several uses of the word. Of special
interest is his article "On Dialectic," which, incidentally,
Boli-Bennett could not use in his own article for the simple
reason that it was written a year later than his own. After
this, we shall look at Ellul's dialectic from three different
but related perspectives: dialectic as a description of reality,

---

[1]G.F. Hegel, The Logic of Hegel, trans. William Wallace
(Oxford: Clarendon Press, 1892), p. 148.

29

as the apprehension of that reality, and as the key to biblical theology.[2] A conclusion summarizes the chapter.

B. Background

If ever there was a word which had lost all meaning because of notorious use and abuse, that word would be "dialectic," a word which has meant all things to all people. Kenneth Burke, for example, catalogues twelve different uses of the word.[3] More modest is the article by Roland Hall, who proffers eight ideal types, with historical examples to illustrate each one.[4] As for the value of dialectic, beauty is in the eye of the beholder. For some, such as Plato, dialectic yields the most certain knowledge, while for others, such as Aristotle, its results are only probable at best. For medieval thinkers the term dialectic is synonymous with the canons of linear logic, such as the law of non-contradiction. Some people of this persuasion vehemently argue that these canons must be preserved and upheld at any cost. Karl Popper, for example, rejects all approaches which happily embrace contradictions. To embrace contradictions, he suggests, is "totally useless" and entails "a complete breakdown of science."[5] Still others are of the exact opposite opinion. For them, the canons of logic are, at best, insufficient, and, at worst, totally counter-productive. Sidney Hook cites Boris Bogoslovsky as such an example.[6]

---

[2] Boli-Bennett's article, excellent as it is, focuses almost exclusively on the first of these three aspects.

[3] Kenneth Burke, A Grammar of Motives (New York: Meridian, 1962), pp. 403ff.

[4] The Encyclopedia of Philosophy, 1972 reprint edition, s.v. "Dialectic," by Roland Hall.

[5] Karl Popper, "What is Dialectic?" Mind: A Quarterly Review of Psychology and Philosophy 49, no. 196 (October 1940): 408, 410. Because he considers the term to be so dangerously misleading and confusing, Popper would even like to discontinue its use (p. 412).

[6] Sidney Hook, "What is Dialectic?" Journal of Philosophy 26, no. 4 (February 14, 1929): 94. Hook's article is a review of three books about dialectic: Mortimer Adler's Dialectics (1927), Jonas Cohn's Theorie der Dialektik (1923), and Bogoslovsky's The Technique of Controversy; Principles of Dynamic Logic (1928).

According to Hook, Bogoslovsky, "not content with modifying the traditional logic, declares it to be basically unsound and proclaims that the old laws of logic must be replaced with new ones."[7] Thus, as Rescher observes, dialectics has been the alchemy of philosophy, serving its constituents as either the quintessential method of inquiry or the quintessential antimethod.[8]

1. Dialectic Broadly Conceived

When and with whom did dialectic originate? Apart from Ellul's peculiar thesis that the Hebrews of the eighth century B.C. used what later became known as dialectic,[9] most philosophers point to the Greeks of the sixth or fifth century B.C. Some suggest that Heraclitus, with his conception of reality as composed of opposites, contradiction and change, is "the fountainhead of western dialectic."[10]

Aristotle mentions Zeno of Elea, author of the famous paradoxes, as the inventor of dialectic. In this sense, dialectic is the rejection of a hypothesis by forcing the logical consequences of the hypothesis. For example, it is unacceptable that Achilles would never overtake the tortoise and, for that reason, Zeno rejects the hypothesis of motion.

The Sophists gave to dialectic a pejorative connotation. For them dialectic was simply a rhetorical device used to win an argument. Protagoras, most famous of the Sophists, argued that he could, with dialectic, "make the worse argument appear the better."[11] Socrates, on the other hand, gave the word a

---

[7] Ibid.

[8] Nicholas Rescher, Dialectics; A Controversy-Oriented Approach to the Theory of Knowledge (Albany: State University of New York, 1977), p. xi. Rescher narrows his discussion to dialectics conceived as formal disputation, "squarely within the rhetorical tradition whose fountainhead is Aristotle" (p. xi).

[9] Ellul, "On Dialectic," p. 298. Compare his similar statements in The Betrayal of the West, pp. 22-23.

[10] Ernest Koenker, Great Dialecticians in Modern Christian Thought (Minneapolis: Augsburg Publishing House, 1971), p. 16. Koenker, incidentally, is the only other person I have found who, like Ellul, mentions the Hebrews in conjunction with the origin of dialectic. See pp. 13-14 of his book.

[11] The Encyclopedia of Philosophy, ibid., p. 386.

broader and more meaningful definition. For him, it meant the method of question and answer used to seek the truth (and not just to win an argument).

Plato and Aristotle loom large in any discussion of our term. Plato agrees with Socrates, but adds another dimension to it, the idea of "a repeated analysis of genera into species, of more general notions into less general ones."[12] According to Plato, dialectic afforded the surest and most certain form of knowledge. Aristotle, however, relegated dialectic to a lesser status. For him, dialectic was tantamount to syllogistic reasoning, the affirmation of first principles which were generally recognized by everyone, and the criticism of mere sophistical reasoning in its pejorative sense. In contrast to this "logic of probability" stood true scientific knowledge, which through empirical verification was the most certain form of knowing.[13]

From the patristic to medieval period dialectic was synonymous with formal logic and classified as one of the liberal arts of the trivium, along with grammar and rhetoric. The first medieval treatise on logic, for example, by the English scholar and theologian Alcuin, was entitled Dialectica. So defined, the problem arose in theology as to how adequate finite human reason was in its ability to understand and interpret divine revelation, which operated in the realm of faith. According to Michaud-Quantin and Weisheipl this controversy reached its peak in the 11th and 12th centuries with the Eucharist and Trinitarian controversies.[14]

---

[12] Ibid.

[13] For dialectic as conceived by Plato and Aristotle, see the article by J.J. Ziegler, "Dialectics," in The New Catholic Encyclopedia, volume IV (Washington, D.C.: The Catholic University of America, 1967), pp. 843-846. Most of the article is devoted to these two thinkers.

[14] The New Catholic Encylopedia, volume IV (Washington, D.C.: The Catholic University of America, 1967) s.v. "Dialectics in the Middle Ages," by P. Michaud-Quantin and J.A. Weisheipl, p. 846. Pascal, who is often mentioned as a "dialectician," gives trenchant expression to this problem of how finite reason and logic is to grasp truths which, by definition, go beyond the merely finite realm, in his Pensées, #861: "Faith embraces many truths which seem to contradict each other." Compare Pensées #267, 384, and 253. Tertullian, for whom the incarnation is certain because it is impossible (certum est quia impossibile), is probably the first and most famous theologian to state the
(footnote continued on following page)

Moving to more modern times, Kant generalized in his Critique of Pure Reason that the so-called dialectics of the ancients was but a "logic of illusion." For Kant, dialectic meant the critique of such disastrous illusions and the attempt to show that the finite human mind is bound to this earthly realm of phenomena. It has no ability to pierce the realm of the noumenal. Thus, for him, dialectic implied a sort of catharsis of the mind.

While Fichte seems to have been the first to make explicit use of thesis, antithesis, and synthesis,[15] Hegel gave dialectic its impetus in modern times and invested it with a new meaning. Prior to him, with the possible exception of Heraclitus, dialectic was a method by which, in various ways, to apprehend reality. That is, it was a mode of thought. Hegel, however, meant that dialectic was also a description of reality itself. According to him, the real, seen as Absolute Spirit's unfolding of and return to itself, was composed of necessary and inherent oppositions or contradictions. By focusing on Geist, commentators have referred to his dialectic as conceptual, spiritual, or cognitive.[16]

Marx converted Hegel's spiritual dialectic into a material one by substituting matter for spirit. Concurring with Hegel that contradictions and oppositions inhere in the very nature of reality, he nevertheless argued that these contradictions resided in the material, not the spiritual, conditions of life. That is, the material conditions the ideal, and not vice versa as Hegel said. Oppositions such as class antagonism characterize material life and serve to force the progress of history, as each stage gives rise to the next.

The dialectics of Hegel and Marx might be described as

---

[14] (cont'd) ...problematic relationship between faith and reason so boldly: "I believe because it is absurd" (credo quia est absurdum).

[15] The Encyclopedia of Philosophy, ibid., p. 387. Sidney Hook rightly points out, though, that the actual use of these three technical terms is "the least significant aspect of the dialectical method." See his book From Hegel to Marx (London: Victor Gollanez Ltd., 1936), p. 61. On pp. 60-76 Hook provides an overview of "The Dialectic Method in Hegel and Marx."

[16] On Hegel's dialectic, see Popper's article, mentioned above in footnote #5, pp. 413-421, and Hook's book, mentioned in footnote #15.

"ascending,"[17] or "synthetic,"[18] in that they both foresee an ultimate unity of all contradictions. Citing Gurvitch, Boli-Bennett observes, "By a series of resolutions of contradictions, history finally arrives (for Hegel) at perfect Freedom enthroned in the state or (for Marx) at the classless communist society where the basic contradiction between thesis (the bourgeoisie) and antithesis (the proletariat) yields to the transcending triumph of the latter."[19]

2. Dialectic and Theology

When we turn to the use of dialectic in theology, the situation is no less complex or confusing. Here too it means all things to all people. Apart from the particular historical manifestation of "dialectical theology" early in our century, a tradition in which Ellul follows, the term has been used to describe thinkers who span the theological spectrum. Barth even uses the word to describe Schleiermacher's theology.[20]

We have already mentioned the 11th and 12th century Eucharist and Trinitarian controversies between the "dialecticians"

---

[17]Georges Gurvitch, Dialectique et sociologie (Paris: Flammarion, 1962), pp. 156. Cited by Boli-Bennett in his article, p. 174.

[18]Jacob Taubes, "Dialectic and Analogy," Journal of Religion 34 (April 1954): 117. Taubes distinguishes between Hegel's "dialectic of synthesis" and Kierkegaard's "dialectic of antithesis." Others make similar distinctions. Mondin refers to Hegel's dialectic as "optimistic" and Kierkegaard's as "pessimistic." See his article, "Dialectic in Theology," The New Catholic Encyclopedia, p. 842. Koenker, p. 156, suggests that there are two main types of dialectic, those which emphasize opposition (Luther, Pascal, Kierkegaard, Barth, and Elert), and those which stress mediation or reconciliation (Hegel and Tillich). This will become an important distinction in our Chapter Five.

[19]John Boli-Bennett, "The Absolute Dialectics of Jacques Ellul," in Paul T. Durbin, ed., Research in Philosophy and Technology, Volume 3 (Greenwich, C.T.: JAI Press, 1980), p. 174.

[20]Karl Barth, The Theology of Schleiermacher, ed., Dietrich Ritschl, trans. Geoffrey Bromiley (Grand Rapids: Eerdmans, 1982), pp. 78, 150, 153. One cannot but help recall, in this connection, Schleiermacher's own Dialectics, first published posthumously in 1839.

34

and their opponents, the grammarians and the monks. Mondin goes so far as to suggest that dialectic has been used "by almost every Protestant theologian" since Hegel and Kierkegaard.[21] One is tempted to agree, and even to eliminate his chronological restrictions. Koenker, for example, applies the term in his book to Augustine, Pseudo-Dionysius, John Scotus Erigena, Meister Eckhardt, Abelard, Aquinas, Nicholas Cusanus, Giordano Bruno, Luther, Jacob Boehme, Pascal, Hegel, Kierkegaard, Barth, Tillich, Heidegger, Bultmann, and Werner Elert.[22] While it may not be inaccurate to apply the term to these thinkers, it does render the word "dialectic" unnecessarily vague by reducing their similarities of thought to the smallest common denominator. Because it is beyond the scope or purpose of this work to untangle this knotty problem, and because Ellul himself fits nicely into a particular theological tradition, we shall restrict our remarks to the rise of dialectical theology early in our century.

Except for Kierkegaard, who as one born before his time directed attention to the qualitative abyss between the Wholly Other God and finite man, the idea of the continuity of all life, not its discontinuity, characterized not only 19th century liberal theology, but 19th century culture in general. Spurred on in particular by Darwin's Origin of Species (1859), theology sought for what Daniel Williams calls the "organic unity" between Christianity and the evolutionary world view.[23] Kenneth Cauthen refers to the same thing when he mentions the "monism" of the period which emphasized that "reality is fundamentally one realm, one process, one structure of activities."[24]

In a world view like this, Christianity was not seen as <u>sui</u>

---

[21]Mondin, ibid.

[22]I have taken all these examples from throughout Koenker's book.

[23]Daniel Day Williams, God's Grace and Man's Hope (New York: Harper and Brothers, 1949), p. 22.

[24]Kenneth Cauthen, The Impact of American Religious Liberalism (New York: Harper and Row, 1962), p. 209. Cauthen also refers to "the pervasive principle of continuity" which typified the liberal theology of that day (p. 110). Lloyd Averill provides one other documentation of this idea in his book, American Theology in the Liberal Tradition (Philadelphia: Westminster Press, 1967), p. 70: "The world view of the liberal was shaped by the theory of evolution, with its view of the continuity of all life."

generis, but simply as one instance of a universal phenomenon. Theological examples of this theme of the continuity of all life abound: the continuity between man and nature, nature and super-nature (Troeltsch and the rise of the study of comparative religions), church and culture, revelation and religion (the rational intelligibility of all truth; the rise of historical criticism), and between this life and the next (eschatology[25]).

Only when viewed against this historical background does the full import of the reaction against liberal theology by "dialectical" theology make sense. The rise of dialectical theology began with the shattering impact of World War I and was given its most vigorous expression in Barth's Römerbrief. Others closely associated with the movement included Friedrich Gogarten, Emil Brunner, Eduard Thurneysen, and Bultmann. In 1922, Barth, Gogarten and Thurneysen founded the journal Zwischen den Zeiten as the primary instrument to express their new ideas. Major tenets of the "dialecticians" included God's aseity as Wholly Other, the infinite, qualitative difference between God and man, time and eternity, the absolute discontinuity between the biblical revelation and reason or religion, and the exclusivity of Jesus Christ. Its "dialectic," therefore, required the critical negation of man's efforts at establishing this continuity of all life and the maintenance of a tension between God's No and Yes. In contrast to the previous century, then, it stressed heterogeneity, not homogeneity, in the God-man relationship. By 1926-27 the movement splintered, with its members differing on the proper nature of its agenda. Bouillard suggests that Gogarten's joining with the "German Christians" in 1933, and the famous Barth-Brunner debate on natural theology in 1934, mark the terminus ad quem of the movement as a cohesive whole.[26]

---

[25]See, for example, Walter Rauschenbusch, A Theology for the Social Gospel (Nashville: Abingdon, 1981), pp. 232-235.

[26]Sacramentum Mundi, volume II (New York: Herder and Herder, 1968), s.v. "Dialectical Theology," by Henri Bouillard, p. 78. For a fuller treatment of the movement, see James Robinson, ed., The Beginnings of Dialectical Theology (Richmond: John Knox Press, 1968), and Thomas Finger, "Dialectical Theology's View of Reason" (PhD dissertation, Claremont Graduate School, 1975). Barth recounts his personal relation to liberal theology in general, and to Schleiermacher in particular, in his "Concluding Unscientific Postscript," which, incidentally, is notable for its much more irenic tone. For a Catholic critique, see Hans Urs von Balthasar, The Theology of Karl Barth, trans. John Drury (New York: Holt, Rinehart, and Winston, 1971), pp. 48-73, entitled "Dialectical Theology."

C. Ellul on Dialectic

Ellul operates within the theological tradition which we have just described. We reviewed in the last chapter his relationship to Barth. Nevertheless, his own use of dialectic is not strictly confined to this movement, but instead moves beyond it even as it incorporates it. Apart from the many scattered references to dialectic in his books, his only article on the subject is his "On Dialectic." In this section we shall use this as a basis of discussion, as we cull out from his other books what he means. In the next section we shall synthesize and illustrate the matter more fully.

Ellul attempts to explain his dialectical method for two reasons: he finds that many Americans are unfamiliar with it, and, more importantly, "dialectic has a central place" for him. [27] In a general sense, dialectic means not only a dialogue or exchange (dialegein), such as that which Ellul invites with his readers, but also opposition or contradiction. Simply put, "dialectics is a procedure that does not exclude contraries, but includes them."[28] We observe dialectic not only in reality (Ellul gives the example of a positive and negative charge producing a flash), but also in thought.

1. General Description

Most important for Ellul is his contention that dialectic "always claims to have to do with the real, to be a means of taking account of the real."[29] By the very nature of the case, then, any mode of thought must take into account this fact of reality, that in the very nature of things contradictory factors co-exist, positive and negative elements which do not cancel out each other but interact so as to modify each other. Hence, for Ellul, dialectic is both a mode of thinking or way of knowledge, and a description of "the real in history" or reality itself. History itself advances by means of a dialectic, and anyone who would think about it must take this into account.

Ellul makes two other points worth noting. First, the opposing or contradictory elements in reality have a wholly positive function. In Hegel's words, there is a positivity in the negative. That is, for Ellul, dialectical tension, change,

---

[27] Ellul, "On Dialectic," p. 292.

[28] Idem, POOA, p. 7.

[29] Idem, "On Dialectic," p. 293.

or historical ambivalence, the coexistence of mutually opposing elements, all constitute the sine qua non of a healthy society. Nothing could be more perilous than cultural sclerosis, monotony, or uncontested and forced conformity. The absence of fruitful dialectic characterizes, say, a totalitarian or utopian society, according to Ellul. In both of these there is a suppression or absence of any conditions for change, for a transition to a possibly better situation.[30] In this sense we can understand Ellul's statement about there not being enough chaos or tension in society.[31] According to him, the best thing that could happen to society would be increased disorder. The problem with technique is its homogenizing tendency which totally eliminates any and all heterogeneity, lack of conformity, or minority position. To put it another way, this dialectic, which society requires to be healthy, places a premium on human initiative and choices. It insists that people have a strategic part to play in making history, and that dialectic "implies the certitude of human responsibility and therefore a freedom of choice and decision."[32]

Our second point is that the ultimate source of Ellul's commitment to dialectic rests in his belief that it is found in the Bible. Indeed, as we have already mentioned, according to Ellul, the true progenitors of dialectic are the Hebrews of the eighth century B.C. For Ellul, "only dialectical thinking can give a proper account of scriptural revelation, such revelation itself being fundamentally and intrinsically dialectical."[33]

---

[30] I underline the word "possibly" because for Ellul the advance to a new stage may or may not entail what we would call true progress. He differs in this respect from Hegel and Marx for whom the synthesis of opposing factors entailed a necessarily better, superior stage. This is by no means a given for Ellul.

[31] See "Between Chaos and Paralysis," p. 747, and ISOS, p. 195.

[32] Ellul, "On Dialectic," p. 297. We see, then, how misguided are the accusations against Ellul which accuse him of fatalism. According to Ellul, fate operates only when people give up.

[33] Ibid., p. 304. Cf. POOA, pp. 8-9. For two excellent treatments of Ellul's doctrine of Scripture, see David Gill's "Jacques Ellul's View of Scripture," Journal of the Evangelical Theological Society 25, no. 4 (December 1982): 467-78, and Temple's dissertation, pp. 197-309.

We could give scores of examples of dialectic in the Bible, but shall limit ourselves in this section to the five instances he mentions in his article "On Dialectic." (1) God who is beyond time and history enters human history, becoming man's partner in dialogue. The incarnation best expresses this, as does the unfolding of God's relation to his people in the process of command-disobedience-judgement-reconciliation. Ellul has devoted an entire book to this subject, rationally insoluble, of the inter-relation of divine sovereignty and human responsibility, or what Barth calls the free determination of man in the free decision of God.[34]

(2) There is a dialectical relation between the eschatological Already and the Not Yet, in the constant renewal of promise and fulfillment. (3) We observe in the Bible a dialectical relation between the whole and the remnant, the simultaneous reduction of election to one man, Jesus, and its expansion in the recapitulation of all things and the universal salvation of all people.[35]

(4) Paul, whose theology is "essentially dialectical" according to Ellul, presents a dialectic between salvation by grace alone (Ephesians 2:8-9) and human works (Philippians 2:12-13). (5) Finally, Ellul gives the example of the relation of History to the Parousia. The former is by no means unimportant or negligible, but it does, nevertheless, move towards decisive judgement and catastrophe.

2. The function of Ellul's particular dialectic

In several places Ellul has described how this general conception of dialectic takes particular shape in his own work and method. Of primary importance for understanding him is what he calls his "double conversion" to Marx and Christianity. Man exists simultaneously in two realms, as matter and spirit, and, for that reason, one must study him as such. Marx convinced Ellul of the necessity of a rigorous, strictly scientific study of the material conditions which shape our lives. Ellul's commitment to biblical revelation, however, led him to study man as a spiritual being. According to Ellul, these two perspectives can neither be separated nor synthesized. Their only proper

---

[34] See Ellul's The Judgement of Jonah, pp. 24, 35, and his entire book The Politics of God and the Politics of Man.

[35] Ellul, "On Dialectic," p. 301.

relation is dialectical and mutually critical.[36]

On the one hand, these two tracks of study are separated, a point which both Ellul and others make.[37] By this Ellul means that his social scientific studies stand on their own and do not require a position of Christian faith to validate them. In other words, his sociological studies do not depend on his theological biases. On the other hand, although the two tracks are separated in this sense, they form a whole with the theological track related necessarily to the sociological track. The two tracks, therefore, constitute "two factors both alien and yet indissolubly bound to one another."[38] They are separate but reciprocally related.

This reciprocal relation between his sociological and theological works is not one of mere complementation, but one of correlation, confrontation, and mutual criticism. Sociology, on the one hand, serves a critical function on behalf of theology in at least three ways. First, it forces theology to be timely and relevant, by identifying for it the pertinent questions and strategic factors which shape modern culture. Ellul, obviously, contends that technique is the constitutive element of our modern culture. It has replaced the role and function which capital had in Marx's own scheme. Too often theology asks the wrong questions, or questions which are antiquated. Sociology can help to prevent this mistake by theology.

Second, sociology forces theology to be not only relevant, but also concrete. According to Ellul, another pitfall into which theology falls, especially dialectical theology which stresses God's transcendence, is its tendency to drift off into the heavens, into the realm of the purely abstract or ideal. Ellul excoriates Barth for this.[39] Like Kierkegaard, Ellul tends to minimize theology which functions only as an academic

---

[36]See POOA, pp. 15, 91, ISOS, pp. 15-18, and "Mirror of These Ten Years," pp. 200-201.

[37]See ISOS, p. 181, and "On Dialectic," pp. 305-306: "Each work would have to be exactly equal and as immune as possible from contamination by the other." Cf. also Katharine Temple's article "The Sociology of Jacques Ellul," in Research in Philosophy and Technology, volume 3, 1980, p. 253.

[38]Ellul, "On Dialectic," p. 306.

[39]Jacques Ellul, The Ethics of Freedom, pp. 456-460, 501 and footnote #86.

enterprise concerned with doctrine, and to maximize its relation to concrete, real-life existence.

Third, sociology forces the church to examine itself and to determine the degree to which it is functioning as a purely sociological group without any truly Christian distinctives. That is, it can help the church to avoid blatant conformity to the world. Two of the most unfortunate examples of such sociological conformity to the world, according to Ellul, are the World Council of Churches and liberation theology. Both come under his heavy fire. Ellul does not mean to say that sociological factors alone determine the church's existence, but only that sometimes it is hard to tell in what ways the church is truly unique.[40]

Theology, on the other hand, also serves to confront sociology. Simply put, it forces sociology to be wholistic. Many sociologists want to remain "purists" and to disavow any interest in values or meaning. Their only domain is a neutral appraisal of sociological phenomena which results in mathematical results. Ellul cites Gurvitch as an example. In addition to being unrealistic and idealistic, the unfortunate tendency of this approach, says Ellul, is that sociology tends to become reductionistic, defining man, for example, only by such things as his work (homo faber) or by his economic activity (homo oeconomicus). By focusing solely on the material, sociology neglects the equally important spiritual nature of people.[41] For Ellul, Christianity provides this complementary set of values.

3. Ellul's overall corpus

Thus, with a methodological plan devised as early as 1942-43, and from which he has never departed, Ellul can say that "the sum of my books constitutes a whole consciously

---

[40] Ellul devotes an entire chapter of FPOK to this matter (pp. 72-86). One example of his own attempt to examine the church from this sociological perspective is his article "On the Cultural and Social Factors Influencing Church Division," Ecumenical Review 4 (April 1952): 269-275.

[41] This is one of Ellul's primary criticisms of Marx. Marx provided him with excellent guidance in understanding the importance of how material factors shape human lives (although the factors have changed since his time), but he had nothing whatsoever to offer Ellul in understanding what Ellul calls the existential questions of life, death, love, and so on.

41

conceived as such."[42]   A result of this dialectical method is
that those who would understand Ellul are forced to digest not
one or two of his books, but a dozen or so.   As Boli-Bennett
observes, "As demanding a task as it may be, his work really
must be read in its entirety or not at all."[43]   Failure to
read broadly in Ellul's corpus almost always results in
misconstruing his intent.   To read, for example, only his
sociological works on technique and politics understandably
leads one to infer that he is a fatalist of sorts.   This,
however, is entirely misleading, for it neglects an entire pole
of the dialectic.[44]   A reading of Ellul's theological works on
the biblical revelation, with its promise of universal salvation, reveals his unbounded optimism which absolutely prohibits
despair.   Thus we can illustrate the direct, dialectical
relation of several of his books by the following diagram:

SOCIOLOGICAL STUDIES   BIBLICAL-THEOLOGICAL STUDIES

The Technological Society   The Meaning of the City[45]

---

[42]Ellul, "On Dialectics," p. 304.

[43]Boli-Bennett, p. 197. Ellul makes a similar comment in
ISOS, p. 193.

[44]Jacob Taubes shows how Barth's dialectical method
suffered a similar fate at the hands of his critics. Those who
focused on one pole of his dialectic accused him of a Manichean
dualism, while those who focused on the other pole accused him
of pantheism or theopantheism. Need we recall that, by
definition, dialectic, as Barth and Ellul use it, requires us to
hold two opposing factors in tension without separating them or
neglecting either pole? See Jacob Taubes, "Theodicy and
Theology: A Philosophical Analysis of Karl Barth's Dialectical
Theology," Journal of Religion 34 (October 1954): 238.

[45]According to Ellul, the city is the purest form of
technique, "the absolute synthesis of all that is worldly" (The
Meaning of the City, p. 20), and, at the same time, the model of
the eschaton, seen in Revelation's depiction of Jerusalem.

42

The Technological System   Apocalypse[46]

The Political Illusion   The Politics of God...and Man
                                    False Presence of the Kingdom

AN INDICATIVE ETHICS AS THE FINAL GOAL OF THE DIALECTIC

To Will and to Do

The Ethics of Freedom[47]

D. Synthesis and Illustrations

In an attempt to synthesize the above material on Ellul's
dialectical method, in this section we will summarize his views
according to three perspectives or levels. Keep in mind that
these three categories are not mutually exclusive, nor are they
used by Ellul himself. They simply serve as a descriptive tool
to understand Ellul's multifaceted use of dialectic in his
method.

1. Dialectic as a description of reality: the phenomenological

It is not without reason that Temple, in her dissertation,
uses the rather unlikely designation "phenomenologist" to

---

[46]See Apocalypse, p. 13, where Ellul suggests that this
commentary "attempts to set forth the dialectical position I can
have in regard to society, human works, and especially
technique, for the confrontation between the sociological
reality and the reading of an example."

[47]Ellul describes the goal of his entire corpus as "an
ethic stemming from a biblical theology." See ISOS, p. 186.
This ethic can be only indicative, relative, and hortatory, and
never rigid or absolute. See To Will and to Do, p. 252.

describe Ellul.[48] By this she does not at all mean that Ellul
subscribes to anything like that technical school of philosophy
which goes by that name. Instead, she wants to draw attention
to Ellul's intense concern to describe the real, the "phenomena"
of every day life. Thus, over and over again Ellul disclaims
any interest or ability in abstract philosophizing. He wants to
avoid at all costs any form of idealism.[49] Instead, he
presumes to take the posture of the ordinary man in the street,
and he purposes to write not about ideas but about his experiences.[50] This emphasis on concrete, material reality, says
Ellul, was one of the three lasting influences which Marx had on
him.[51]

   As we indicated in the last section, according to Ellul,
the key to understanding this reality is to recognize its
dialectical character. In some places he describes this

---

[48]See chapter II of her dissertation, entitled "Fact,
Reality, the Sacred and Myth."

[49]Berthoud is wrong, therefore, when he writes, "toute
l'oeuvre de Jacques Ellul ait été piégée dans l'idéalisme
philosophique." See page 190 of his article. It is precisely
this philosophical idealism which Ellul seeks to avoid at all
costs.

[50]Ellul, ISOS, pp. 188-190, and 219-220. Another good
example of this attitude of Ellul's is the very first paragraph
of his book The Humiliation of the Word, trans. Joyce Hanks
(Grand Rapids: Eerdmans, 1985): "Don't look here for some
scholarly study on iconic expression or syntagmatics or
metalanguage. I am not pretending to push forward scientific
frontiers. Rather, I try to do here the same thing I do in all
my books: face, alone, this world I live in, try to understand
it, and confront it with another reality I live in, but which is
utterly unverifiable. Taking my place at the level of the
simplest of daily experiences, I make my way without critical
weapons. Not as a scientist, but as an ordinary person, without
scientific pretensions, talking about what we all experience, I
feel, listen, and look." Hereafter cited as Humiliation.

[51]Idem, POOA, p. 11. Ellul does not, however, subscribe
to any form of materialism, which, in his eyes, would simply be
another ideology. See Boli-Bennett, p. 186, where he observes
that Ellul agrees with Hegel that reality itself is dialectical
in nature, but agrees with Marx that this dialectic is not
merely spiritual but concrete and material.

dialectic within reality as the movement of history.[52]
Boli-Bennett's article focuses on this aspect of Ellul's
dialectic, and we review it briefly here.

Dialectical relationships constitute "the very fabric of
life...the very core of reality" for Ellul.[53] Boli-Bennett
suggests that there are five major components to Ellul's
dialectic of social reality. There is dialectical tension
between ideology and reality, action and consequences, the whole
and the parts,[54] the radical ambivalence of action, and
between social and spiritual reality. In addition, from the
theological perspective, dialectical tension exists at the point
of Ellul's idea of the sacred-desacralization-resacralization
progression, and between God's Yes and No.

The present danger to society, according to Ellul, is the
elimination of these dialectical tensions which are not at all
inevitable and which constitute the very possibility and
definition of history. Boli-Bennett, Konrad Kellen, Temple,
Menninger and others have all recognized this point.[55] The
dialectical interplay of various material factors constitutes
the very warp and woof of history, according to Ellul. In his
commentary Apocalypse, for example, Ellul suggests that the book
of Revelation is the book of all human history. This history is
not the product of mechanistic causality or of mere chance, but
the dialectical interplay of the will of the Lord, the will of
men, and certain "abstract forces."[56] Later in this book
Ellul specifies five concrete components of this dialectic:
political power, economic power, forces of destruction and
negation, the Word of God, the prayers of his people, and the
setting apart of God's people.

A healthy society, then, according to Ellul, one in which
history is truly possible, is one which is full of dialectical
tensions. These tensions introduce elements of flexibility,

---

[52]See ISOS, pp. 201-202, and Humiliation, p. 254.

[53]Boli-Bennett, p. 171.

[54]Compare the similar distinction which I make in
Chapter III, footnote #29.

[55]See Boli-Bennett (pp. 191-192), Temple's article, "The
Sociology of Jacques Ellul" (pp. 238-240), Kellen's Translator's
Introduction to The Political Illusion, and Menninger's
dissertation (p. 189).

[56]Ellul, Apocalypse, p. 146.

mobility, fluidity and uncertainty. Human action and initiative then take on real importance and effect. The quest for a "utopia" of any sort exemplifies a most unfortunate attempt to eliminate these dialectical tensions.[57] Just as in a totalitarian state, utopias remove all creative contradictions, all possibilities for individuality and uniqueness. A utopia, Ellul suggests, would signify the end of history, for it would be the most monotonous and boring of all worlds, the epitome of utter, preplanned and unrelenting conformity, a place where all people would be adapted and integrated into a monistic whole. Those who would contribute to a healthy society and to the possibility of history, then, would not seek to eliminate tensions, but to reintroduce them in the most fruitful manner possible.[58]

2. Dialectic as the apprehension of reality: the epistemological

Dialectic occurs in Ellul's method at another level and in a different sense, at what I call the epistemological level. That is, for Ellul, not only is reality itself dialectical, but so is our means for apprehending that reality. Some confusion exists whether Ellul does indeed use dialectic as an epistemological tool. Temple writes, for example, "It is important to note that Ellul does not see dialectics as a specific mode of reasoning, but rather as a description of the relationships involved in the way things are."[59] Ellul even makes a similar remark in one of his articles.[60] The point at issue seems to be Ellul's relation to Hegel. Ellul rejects the Hegelian notion of a purely spiritual dialectic, and sides with Marx that it is instead a material dialectic. Our last section above concentrated on this level of Ellul's dialectic. Yet this does not mean that Ellul rejects dialectic on the epistemological level. He simply rejects the idea that dialectic is only conceptual.

In his article "On Dialectic," Ellul explicitly affirms that there are two aspects to dialectic--"a dialectic of ideas,

---

[57]See Ellul's The Betrayal of the West, trans. Matthew J. O'Connell (New York: Seabury, 1978), pp. 147-169. Hereafter cited as Betrayal.

[58]For an example of such, see Ellul's The Political Illusion, trans. by Konrad Kellen (New York: Knopf, 1967), pp. 206-223.

[59]Temple, "The Sociology of Jacques Ellul," p. 238.

[60]Jacques Ellul, "Work and Calling," Katallagete: Be Reconciled 4 no. 3 (Fall-Winter 1972): 15.

but perhaps also a dialectic of facts, of reality."[61] In his autobiographical work, In Season, Out of Season, this becomes even clearer:

> It is true that there is a dialectic within my work, and it is entirely central in that I have discovered progressively that in the world we live in there are no means of thinking and acquiring knowledge that are not of a dialectical nature...I became conscious, as I worked and thought, that I needed to interpret all things in a dialectical manner.[62]

In this same work Ellul describes the dialectical interplay of his sociological and biblical perspectives as akin to Mao's statement about walking on two legs.[63]

In addition to this dialectic between his sociology and theology, which we examined in the last section and saw in the relation of his books to each other, Ellul's epistemology is dialectical in at least two other ways. First, as Menninger points out in his interview, Ellul is willing, at times, to reject linear logic as a fully adequate tool.[64] Ellul agrees with this accusation, although several points are worth noting. Ellul does not at all disparage human reason or logic as useless. He only wants to curtail the hubris which sometimes is associated with its use, its pretense to understand and explain everything, and its tendency to leave no room for the unexplained mystery. As Temple puts it,

> Reason, in short, [for Ellul] is a relative faculty, but not a nonfaculty. In order to confront reality, people need to use reason...To give up the function of reason altogether leads to the retreat into the irrational. At the same time, he warns against the tendency to try to force reason to exceed its limits.

---

[61]Idem, "On Dialectic," p. 293. Dialectic, therefore, is a mode of thought, but not only a mode of thought. It is also a mode of life and history.

[62]Idem, ISOS, pp. 201-202. Cf. Betrayal, pp. 22-23. Menninger does recognize and affirm that, for Ellul, dialectic functions in both an epistemological, as a mode of thought, and a phenomenological, as a description of reality, fashion. See his dissertation, pp. 67-68.

[63]Ibid., p. 18.

[64]Menninger, pp. 223-224.

Reason becomes de-raison when it oversteps its bounds to claim that everything can be totally explicated by reason. The rigorous use of reason avoids the extremes of the irrational fallacy and the rational-istic fallacy.[65]

Further, Ellul requires that rational logic must always be accompanied by and subsumed under the revelation of God's word,which revelation is often, to use Kierkegaard's words, an absolute paradox which offends human reason (see Philosophical Fragments).

Secondly, Ellul's mode of thinking is dialectical in one other way, in the Socratic sense of the word. Like Kierkegaard, all his writings have a maieutic function. That is, Ellul intends to provoke a critical dialogue and to engage his readers, with the goal of forcing them to make decisions.[66] Like Socrates and Kierkegaard, Ellul adamantly refuses to provide readymade answers, and instead purposes to force his reader to make his own choices.[67] Further, the Socratic dialectic entails the critical examination of commonly held beliefs, beliefs which often have no more support than that of popular opinion or tradition. Ellul, acting the part of the Socratic expert or intellectual gadfly, attempts to help people to discover their own shallow thinking and lack of true critical awareness. To the extent that the Socratic dialectic is "a continuing quest for truth by constant critical analysis, inter-rogation, self-examination, and further analysis,"[68] we can

---

[65]Temple, "The Sociology of Jacques Ellul," p. 225. Compare Pascal's Pensées #253: "Two extremes: to exclude reason, to admit reason only." For a fuller treatment of Ellul's ideas on the nature and role of reason, see Temple's dissertation, pp. 108-159. In Humiliation (pp. 216-217), Ellul even praises the rigor of logical analysis, in contrast to thinking which proceeds on the mere level of intuition and image.

[66]See Humiliation, p. 38. Ellul is in constant dialogue with the reader.

[67]See Frederick Sontag, A Kierkegaard Handbook (Atlanta: John Knox Press), pp. 91-97, who notes the "Socratic" aspect of Kierkegaard's work.

[68]Peter Angeles, Dictionary of Philosophy (New York: Harper and Row, 1981), p. 264.

say that Ellul's own dialectical mode of thought is indeed Socratic.[69]

3. Dialectic as the key to the Bible: the theological

Any discussion of Ellul's dialectic which fails to examine it from the theological or biblical perspective is inadequate. Boli-Bennett's article is weak in this respect, for he devotes almost the entire article to a discussion of Ellul's dialectic on the sociological level. For Ellul, the Bible is the prototype for all dialectic, for dialectic "is specifically a biblical concept," in contrast to philosophical thinking which tends to resolve and to synthesize contradictions.[70] For Ellul, the biblical or theological dialectic operates on both of the levels we have just discussed: it is both a mode of thought, an epistemological orientation by which we interpret scripture, and a mode of Christian existence within reality itself.

In addition to the five examples of Ellul's biblical dialectic which he gives in his article and which we mentioned above, several others show how radical and thoroughgoing is his approach. Ellul interprets the Bible as a whole, each of its separate books, and individual topics in it in a dialectical manner. His works on 2 Kings and the book of Revelation exemplify his approach to whole books. Apocalypse, for example, stands in dialectical relation to other books in his corpus.

---

[69]Several caveats apply to this comparison of Ellul's dialectical epistemology with the Socratic method. Like Kierkegaard, Ellul categorically rejects all forms of idealism. To the extent that Socrates represents the epitome of speculative idealism in, for example, Kierkegaard's Philosophical Fragments, Ellul is decidedly un-Socratic. Further, Ellul's similarity to the Socratic dialectic is only a formal comparison, and not a material one. That is, the intent of Ellul's method, not the method itself or the end result of the method is Socratic. Finally, Ellul never comes close to suggesting that Truth resides latently and eternally within a person, and that through a rational dialogue it is given birth. We do not arrive at Truth by our own initiative through a doctrine of Recollection, but only by God's initiative to us in his revelation. Like Kierkegaard, Ellul would insist that true critical thought becomes possible only after a rebirth through an encounter with the Wholly Other God.

[70]Ellul, Humiliation, p. 253.

49

The text itself, in its structure, movement, organization, and its relation to culture, is read dialectically.[71]

What about particular examples of individual subjects or themes in Scripture? Four examples stand out. First, Ellul's scathing comments on natural or positive law lead one to think that he is a juridical iconoclast. A closer reading, though, reveals that he considers civil law to be ordained by God, serving not only a useful but indispensable function.[72] A relationship exists between divine and human law which prohibits any dichotomy between the two. The Christian has a unique, "double attitude" to civil law.[73] On the one hand, he recognizes that it has been appointed by God, yet, on the other hand, he does not imagine that civil law can or does represent true justice or goodness. In other words, human law exists as what Ellul calls "an intermediate entity" between God's original covenant with people and the final eschaton. It is a relative institution, but not merely relative, "because God endows it with dignity."[74] Only the dialectical perspective does justice to both perspectives.

Closely related to this is Ellul's stance on the state. Here we see "the biblical perspective [which] sees the state as ordained by God, in harmony with the divine order, and at the same time as the Beast of the Abyss, the Great Babylon."[75] Most people are quick to point out passages which justify the state's existence. Ellul does not deny these passages, but would direct our attention to the other pole of the dialectic which maintains a tension. Passages like 1 Samuel 8, Zechariah 11:6, Ecclesiastes, Matthew 4:9 and 23:4, and 1 Corinthians 15:24 all cast the state in a somewhat "negative" light and challenge its validity. Ellul's dialectical reading of

---

[71] Idem, _Apocalypse_, pp. 52-54. In his article on Ellul's view of Scripture (p. 469), Gill observes Ellul's position on the text's relation to culture. In Ellul's words, there is "a complex interplay [=dialectic] of adoption and adaption" which entails the three stages of appropriation, contradiction, and expropriation. See _The Ethics of Freedom_ (p. 164). Gill footnotes an example of this from Ellul's _The Meaning of the City_ (p. 176).

[72] Idem, _The Theological Foundation of Law_, p. 68.

[73] Ibid., p. 100.

[74] Ibid., p. 94.

[75] Idem, _Violence_, p. 2.

50

Scripture affirms both perspectives at once, without trying to synthesize or exclude either.[76] As a result, a Christian's political involvement must involve "a subtle interplay of No and Yes, of approval and rejection, of caution and support, of impulsion and restraint."[77] In short, the biblical dialectic imposes a dialectical existence.

Our third example of Ellul's dialectical treatment of a biblical theme is money. "The Bible," writes Ellul, "contains contradictory texts about wealth."[78] On the one hand, the New Testament seems to condemn it. Ellul finds no passages in the New Testament which justify wealth. Jesus compares Mammon to a god. The Old Testament, on the other hand, "presents wealth as a blessing, willed by God and pleasing to him."[79] In a similar way, in the Old Testament, wealth itself is sometimes portrayed as good, while the wealthy person is often condemned. As Gill points out in the forward to Money and Power, "Ellul's thought and style is thus very dialectical: it highlights the tensions and opposing forces within which God has placed us."[80]

Our last example of Ellul's dialectical interpretation of the Bible is his attitude toward "the world." Ellul is famous for his negativism, and one is tempted to view him as a world-denying pessimist. This reading of Ellul, though, is possible only if one neglects his dialectical interpretation of Scripture on the subject. According to him, we need to observe "the Bible's double affirmation" about the world, that it is at once both lost and loved.[81] On the one hand, the world is the realm of absolute rebellion and radical evil, yet, on the other hand, it retains an infinite value before God because of his irrevocable love. Only a dialectical attitude does full justice to both perspectives.[82] The biblical teaching on the city,

---

[76] Idem, FPOK, pp. 109-117.

[77] Idem, The Ethics of Freedom, pp. 434-435.

[78] Jacques Ellul, Money and Power, trans. LaVonne Neff (Downers Grove, I.L.: Inter-Varsity Press, 1984), p. 35.

[79] Ibid.

[80] David Gill, "Forward," in Money and Power, p. 8.

[81] Ellul, Violence, p. 122.

[82] Idem, "'The World' in the Gospels," Katallagete vol. 5, no. 1 (Spring 1974): 16-23. Contrary to the impression which (footnote continued on following page)

for example, reveals that the city in its present form is the purest form of technique, the epitome of man's self-sufficiency and pride, and, at the same time, the model of the heavenly Jerusalem of the eschaton.[83] Failure to maintain the tension of the dialectic results in unfortunate consequences. Those who stress only its infinite value due to God's love tend to baptize the world without discrimination, while those who only stress its sinfulness often withdraw from it or categorically condemn it. Neither stance is justified, according to Ellul.

As we have said, Ellul's biblical dialectic operates not only as an epistemological tool or mode of thought, as a way to interpret Scripture, but also as a mode of Christian existence within reality. Ellul construes the entire Christian life as a dialectical style of life. "We are invited to take part in a dialectic, to be in the world but not of it."[84] In the metaphor of the city, Christians are implored to be city dwellers, but not city builders, fully participating in its life, but maintaining, as it were, "a dialectic between staying and leaving, preserving and judgement."[85]

Christian existence operates at the juncture or boundary between two realms, the Already and the Not Yet of God's kingdom. This forces the Christian into what Ellul calls an "agonistic" way of life.[86] On the one hand, the Christian cannot accept the world as it is, in all its radical evil and pride, but, on the other hand, one's efforts to change it for good appear to have but a negligible effect. Thus, the Christian lives "at the point of contact between two currents: the will of the Lord, and the will of the world."[87]

---

[82] (cont'd) ...many people have of Ellul, he is not a world-rejecting theologian. As Vahanian shows in his article, "Jacques Ellul and the Religious Illusion," Ellul forces and challenges the Christian to embrace the world (pp. xv, xviii).

[83] See footnote #45 above.

[84] Idem, Violence, p. 26.

[85] Idem, The Meaning of the City, pp. 74-75, 84.

[86] Idem, POK, p. 20.

[87] Ibid., p. 27. Later in this book (p. 44ff.), Ellul uses the classic imagery of dual citizenship in two cities to express the same thing.

We mentioned earlier Ellul's dismay at the progressive elimination of creative and fruitful tensions within society due to the suppressive homogeneity of technique which squeezes everything into its mold. If there is to be any hope of penetrating this otherwise closed, all-embracing system, a factor must be introduced from "above" and "beyond" the system, a factor which cannot be absorbed or assimilated by it. According to Ellul, "this force that the system is incapable of absorbing can only be God, a transcendent God...The only solution left is through a relationship with God."[88]

Christians, through their relationship with this Wholly Other God, are called upon to reintroduce into society the creative tensions which it so badly lacks, and which they alone, as citizens of two realms, can offer. Their role in society is to act as leaven, "to introduce a tension, an element of contradiction and conflict, which replaces the false dialectic of Marx with a true dialectic."[89] By crafting what Ellul calls a unique "style of life" Christians alone can offer to society what it needs the most.

Elsewhere Ellul describes this as the Christian's prophetic vocation, which, by definition, is revolutionary. If the Christian life is not revolutionary, it is nothing, a subversion and betrayal.[90] We mentioned in the last chapter some of the characteristics of such a style of life: the provocation of the status quo, the injection of a presence of the future kingdom into society today,[91] defense of the disenfranchised, the demythologization of society's commonplaces, and the foretelling and warning of consequences for decisions made (cf. Ezekiel). In short, the Christian acts as a fermenting factor, and should, in Ellul's words,

> play the most fruitful, the most positive, the most original role possible: putting the tension into society and thus keeping it alive. He restores society's ability to develop. He offers a truly revolutionary interpretation of life. And it is precisely he alone who can play this role. He causes positive, living, and fruitful contradiction to gush

---

[88] Idem, ISOS, pp. 206-207.

[89] Idem, FPOK, p. 52.

[90] See the entire chapter IV of POK, "Revolutionary Christianity."

[91] See Hope, pp. 231-232.

forth in the heart of a society which prefers to be simplex and which pretends to deny and resolve the contradictions...This contradiction is not something to avoid. It needs rather to be brought out as strongly as possible, not for opposition's sake, but in order that this man, this society, this state, even if one is opposed to them, should live; for without this contradiction they would die.[92]

By definition, the two poles cannot be synthesized or considered autonomous. Neither the world, nor the Biblical revelation in relation to the world, can exist independently. Armed with this dialectical interpretation of scripture, the whole of the Christian's existence revolves around fostering a dialectical tension within the world.

E. Conclusion

In some ways, Ellul's dialectical method is not at all unique. He readily identifies with the concerns of dialectical theology which flourished first with Kierkegaard and then, more formally, in the early decades of the century with Barth. What is unusual is the thoroughgoing extent to which he has self-consciously employed dialectic in his work. As we have seen in numerous examples above, dialectic operates for Ellul as a description of the phenomena of history or reality, as a mode of thought to apprehend this reality (especially in the biblical hermeneutic), and as an existential mode of existence. Sometimes his dialectic is more "negative" or "antithetical," stressing simple oppositions such as the will of the world and the will of the Lord. At other times his emphasis is more "positive," such as when he suggests the mutual criticism which sociology and theology contribute to each other. Further, an important point which we will consider in Chapter 5 will be the extent to which Ellul's dialectic is or is not an "ascending" one, as Gurvitch described those of Marx and Hegel.

Recognizing the importance of Ellul's dialectic is indispensable for appreciating his corpus. In the next two chapters we will show how one particular dialectical theme, the

---

[92] Ellul, To Will and to Do, pp. 107-108. Cf. footnote #35, p. 290 of this book. For another perspective on the dialectical nature of the Christian's existence as a citizen in two worlds, see Vincent Punzo, "Jacques Ellul on the Presence of the Kingdom in the Technological Society," Logos, vol. 1 (1980): 125-137. Punzo suggests that, in Ellul, the Christian's dialectical existence revolves around a knowledge pole, Christian realism, and an action pole, hope.

tension between freedom and necessity, serves as an interpretive key to his many books. Hence, we now move into a more narrow sphere of our concentric circles, from Ellul as an eclectic (Chapter 1), and a dialectician (Chapter 2), to one particular theme which sheds light on the whole and which functions as the kernel of his thought (Chapters 3 and 4).

THE DIALECTIC OF FREEDOM AND NECESSITY AS THE HERMENEUTICAL
KEY TO ELLUL'S THEOLOGICAL METHOD
PART ONE: NECESSITY AS THE NEGATIVE POLE OF THE DIALECTIC

But if, by the operation of necessities of politics and the
laws of society, freedom is necessarily reduced to these
limitations, let us at least be aware that we are staking
the exact opposite of freedom. For what is the meaning of
a freedom that does not allow one to challenge norms and
definitions? What is the meaning of a freedom that does
not allow for the possibility of dissent? What is the
meaning of a freedom that does not recognize the other
person's freedom, with which you come into conflict, and
which may oppose you and threaten to destroy your own?
What is the meaning of a freedom that the free man does not
assume full responsibility for and that he himself does not
defend? What is the meaning of a freedom that does not
involve risk or come into conflict with its opposite? What
is the meaning of a freedom that is not a confrontation of
necessity, and thus, in the political context, a struggle
against its own enemy? It is a parody of freedom.[1]

Jacques Ellul
A Critique of the New Commonplaces

---

[1]Jacques Ellul, A Critique of the New Commonplaces,
trans. Helen Weaver (New York: Knopf, 1968), pp. 169-170.

A. Introduction

Reading Ellul's corpus is not an easy task. Anyone who has attempted to work through one of his books knows that this is true. In Chapter One we observed some of the diverse caricatures of Ellul's work.[2] In addition, we observed several perspectives from which to grasp Ellul's overall methodology in general. When properly defined, for example, we saw that Ellul might well be read as an existentialist, "prophet" or as a theological positivist. Then, in Chapter Two, we saw that his theological method in particular was dialectical.

Ellul, to be sure, is himself partially responsible for the difficulty in reading his work. He has not made the reader's task an easy one. Some of his works are long and tedious. All of them contain a vocabulary and style that bewilder the uninitiated. He has a genius for uncompromising overstatements, absolutistic rhetoric, and a hypercritical attitude. Furthermore, Ellul is anything but systematic. He eschews systematizing for the same reasons and in the same manner that Barth did: systematizing represents an arrogant and ossifying manipulation of the free Word of God.[3] As a result, ambiguities and apparent contradictions abound. Even one of his strengths, his interdisciplinary expertise, contributes to this confusion, for, as Waldo Beach observes, Ellul's mastery of the western intellectual tradition issues forth in a "simplicity of assurance."[4] It is just this assurance which can sound arrogant and condescending.

In Chapter Two we attempted to cut through this interpretive fog. The first step towards understanding Ellul's project, after appreciating his eclectic interests, consists of unpacking what he means by his dialectical method. In Chapters Three and Four we now go a step further. For the reasons cited above

---

[2] See section A, the "Introduction," of Chapter One.

[3] See Stephen Sykes, The Identity of Christianity: Theologians and the Essence of Christianity from Schleiermacher to Barth (Philadelphia: Fortress Press, 1984), p. 199. While Barth seemed singularly unsuccessful at avoiding this perceived pitfall, given his 10,000 page systematic theology, Ellul has been quite successful, for he has written nothing like a systematic theology. His works are somewhat like Luther's, occasional works on the bible and theology.

[4] Waldo Beach, in the "Forward" in To Will and To Do, p. vii.

about the various caricatures which have emerged of Ellul, it would be very helpful to locate a hermeneutical or interpretive key for reading him. These next two chapters propose to do just that. The thesis of these two chapters is that the dialectic between freedom and necessity is the central and controlling idea in all of Ellul's work. This particular focus of his general dialectical method provides his readers with an organizing matrix or paradigm through which one can synthesize nearly all of his works. This freedom/necessity dialectic is, I propose, the golden thread running throughout his corpus, the kernel, or the "essential inspiration"[5] which governs his entire theology.

While we must take seriously Ellul's warning of and distaste for anything that smacks of "systematizing" his work, our present goal is not unwarranted. As Temple observes, we are attempting nothing more than to apply to Ellul's work his own quest to locate the "constituent element" or "main idea" in society.[6] And just as Ellul guards against saying that technique is the only important factor in society, and instead insists that it is the most important one, so we too would argue that while the freedom/necessity dialectic is not the only possible key to his thought, it is, nevertheless, the pivotal one.[7]

---

[5] Wilhelm Niesel, The Theology of Calvin (Grand Rapids: Baker Book House, 1980), p. 9. The reference is obviously to Calvin and not to Ellul. My purpose in chapters Three and Four, though, is quite similar to what Niesel was searching for in Chapter One of his book on Calvin's theology.

[6] Temple, pp. 4-5. For Ellul, the primary factor in our modern society is what he calls "technique." If Marx were alive today, writes Ellul, he would choose technique, not capital, as the constituent element by which to understand society. See POOA, pp. 32, 34.

[7] Ellul discusses the matter of technique as the "determining factor" of society, but not the only factor, in his book The Technological System, trans. Joachim Neugroschel (New York: Continuum, 1980), pp. 51-55. I disagree, then, with Temple, who argues that the dialectic of the two kingdoms is the most important factor in understanding Ellul. I do not deny that this is strategic, but only that the dialectic between the "Already" and the "Not Yet" is the context within which the dialectic between freedom and necessity is worked out.

1. Alternative interpretive keys

Other Ellul interpreters have referred to various ideas of his as "main themes" or "controlling ideas," although none in the formal and sustained manner of these two chapters. Most often such references are made in passing. We saw this on the broader and more general level in Chapter One. On another and more particular level, there are several proposals. According to Burke, Ellul's "christocentric emphasis forms the cornerstone of his entire theology. This point is deceptively simple, but its importance cannot be overlooked."[8] Miller contends that "the Word of God is the central idea of Jacques Ellul's thought." [9] Both of these suggestions are not unreasonable, but they have the disadvantage of not being able to account for the non-Biblical aspects of Ellul's writings. That is, they are strictly theological categories which do not take into account Ellul's sociological interests. In one of the more sustained and convincing suggestions, Temple argues that Ellul's doctrine of the two kingdoms is central. "It is around the nucleus of the two realms that all his writings revolve and find their unity...[It] forms the cornerstone of his thought."[10] Bradley makes a similar assessment, but only in passing.[11]

Of these several suggested interpretive schemes, only Temple goes on to integrate her idea into Ellul's overall thought and show how it operates. As for her own suggestion about the doctrine of the two realms, I would only say that hers is a more general idea which serves to highlight the context in which the more particular dialectic between freedom and necessity is worked out. These two ways of reading Ellul do not at all contradict each other, but rather complement each other in a reciprocal fashion. The goal of Ellul's entire corpus is clearly the formulation of a contemporary Christian ethic. This ethics, to be more exact, is an "ethics of freedom," forged out against the forces of necessity, which the Christian incarnates

---

[8]Burke, p. 57. Compare his similar comment on page 90: "Without a doubt, Ellul's christocentric orientation lies at the core of all his theological writings."

[9]Miller, p. 124.

[10]Temple, pp. 7, 20. Temple does a marvelous job of organizing her entire dissertation around this thesis, showing how the doctrine of the two kingdoms is worked out and evident in Ellul's thought.

[11]Bradley, p. 12.

as a citizen of the two realms, the city of God and the city of man.

Many of Ellul's critics agree with this idea that freedom is the controlling idea in Ellul's work, including Temple herself at one point.[12] Outka acknowledges its "decisive status."[13] Fasching observes that for Ellul, "being human is defined in terms of being free."[14] Burke writes that "the theme of individual liberty unifies Ellul's theological and political writings."[15] Wren comes closest to my own thesis when he writes that "the asphyxiation of individual freedom (especially the freedom to be an individual) and the mutilation of man's psyche by the uncontrolled conditioning of all social life [is] the central theme of Ellul's work."[16]

Ellul himself writes that freedom is at the center of his life and work as a recurring and organizing theme. "Nothing I have done, experienced, or thought makes sense if it is not considered in the light of freedom."[17] Christian liberty is the arena and condition of his proposed ethic,[18] and even the sum and substance of the Christian life.[19] Freedom, he contends, is the universal aspiration of all people every- where,[20] and its neglect by the church helps to explain the

---

[12]Temple, p. 456.

[13]Outka, p. 189.

[14]Fasching, The Thought of Jacques Ellul: A Systematic Exposition, p. 53.

[15]Burke, p. 14.

[16]Wren, p. 5. Compare his similar statements on pages 229-230, 290, and 299.

[17]Ellul, ISOS, p. 183.

[18]Idem, The Ethics of Freedom, p. 7.

[19]Ibid., p. 104. Note page 109: "If there is no freedom there is no Christian life at all. Freedom is preliminary and antecedent to every expression of freedom...It is both the setting in which virtues can develop and also the condition which allows them to exist."

[20]Idem, Betrayal, p. 19.

sadly nominal lifestyles of many.[21] No wonder, then, that he elsewhere writes that "if there is one value which I regard as the most important, it is freedom."[22]

2. Setting the parameters

Before we begin to analyze in depth this freedom/necessity dialectic, two introductory comments are in order. These will help to focus and delimit the ensuing discussion. First, Ellul distinguishes between several levels of reality. On the one hand, for example, we might contemplate reality on a superficial level by, say, analyzing a political speech, press conference, newspaper ad, or a T.V. report. On the other hand, and at the opposite extreme, we might contemplate reality in thoroughly abstract or intellectual terms, such as Ellul criticizes Barth of doing in several instances.[23] Ellul uses the analogy of the ocean with its choppy, everchanging surface, its deep "sepulchral stillness," and the inbetween area of the currents and the tides. In order truly to grasp reality, he suggests, we must avoid the two extremes of superficiality and abstraction, and, instead, examine it at the most realistic level.[24]

---

[21] Idem, The Ethics of Freedom, p. 105.

[22] Idem, "Conformism and the Rationale of Technique," in G.R. Urban and Michael Glenny, eds., Can We Survive Our Future? (New York: St. Martin's Press, 1972), p. 101. When asked by Menninger what was "the principal thing" that he wished to demonstrate to Christians, Ellul responded that "There are two things, actually, which are related: liberty and hope. These are the two lessons that I try to establish in my work." See Menninger interview, p. 220. In personal correspondence with David Gill, Gill confirmed my thesis on the priority of the freedom/necessity dialectic, writing that Ellul "regards freedom/hope (vs. necessity) as the conflict of our time and as the context in which holiness and love get expressed" (David Gill to Dan Clendenin, August 19, 1984). The emphases are his.

[23] See Bromiley's article, JE:IE, p. 46. Bromiley calls this Ellul's "most forthright criticism of Barth." Ellul makes this criticism of Barth in several places. For one example, see The Ethics of Freedom, p. 456, footnote #68, and p. 467.

[24] Ellul, Hope, pp. 279-281. Vincent Punzo observes that Ellul distinguishes between three levels of reality. See his article, p. 128.

Thus, in his discussion of freedom and necessity, we need to distinguish between the metaphysical and the ethical formulations of the problem. Ellul disdains and rejects the former as superficial and abstract. In all his work, he intends to remain "solely on the level of the reality occurring in the world."[25] This is in keeping with his emphasis on what he calls a Christian "realism" (in opposition to any and all forms of "idealism") and the experience-oriented nature of his work.[26] When he considers the factors involved in the freedom/necessity dialectic, therefore, he has no interest whatsoever in what he pejoratively calls the metaphysical formulation of the question, such as whether people are predestined, have a free will or not, and so on. On this level of reality it is what Ellul calls a "false problem" which remains rationally insoluble. According to him, the Bible "does not even ask this [metaphysical] question. The question does not arise."[27] Hence, "it is plain that the real problem of freedom is not metaphysical. The problem of freedom is ethical."[28]

Our second preliminary comment focuses our discussion of the freedom/necessity dialectic even further. Simply put, when Ellul refers to necessity and determinism, he has in mind reality on the collective level, not on the individual level, whereas when he refers to freedom, just the opposite is true. That is, he always considers freedom on the individual level, and never on the collective level. On the one hand, he does not suggest that every individual is equally subject to the deterministic web of society. Any one person may be more or less free. On the collective level, however, the level of the totality of forces, it is impossible to escape the reality of necessity.[29] Freedom, on the other hand, occurs always and

---

[25] Idem, POOA, p. 57.

[26] On Ellul's "Christian realism" see FPOK (p. 171), POOA (p. 11), Hope (pp. 274-282), and ISOS (p. 220). Berthoud has a short section at the end of his article on Ellul's realism.

[27] Ellul, The Ethics of Freedom, p. 76. Compare p. 79.

[28] Ibid., p. 85. Likewise, in his treatise on hope, Ellul warns that his discussion "will not be in the theological or philosophical manner" such as Moltmann's work on the same topic. See Hope, p. vi.

[29] Ibid., p. 42. Two other examples help to illustrate this principle. The problem with technology, as we observed in Chapter One, is not that it is innately bad, a misinterpretation (footnote continued on following page)

only on the individual level. There is no such thing as collective freedom. Freedom, he writes, is "an individual act and lifestyle"[30] for which each person must struggle.

Ellul's discussion of the dialectic between freedom and necessity, therefore, takes place on the ethical rather than on the metaphysical level. Freedom must be discovered and exercised on the individual level as a revolt against the totality of restraints which society imposes on us. With these two preliminary comments in mind, we are now in a position to move on to our more specific discussion of our proposed hermeneutical key to Ellul's method. In the remainder of this Chapter III we will examine the first pole of the dialectic, necessity, while in Chapter IV we shall examine its antithesis, freedom.

B. Ellul's General Prognosis

Mankind today is anything but free. In the words of Rousseau, he is "everywhere in chains." According to Ellul, "the tide of human affairs conveys an element of necessity, a

---

[29] (cont'd) ...which Ellul never tires of rejecting. Nor is the problem that it cannot be used for good. The real problem for Ellul is that technique has formed a system on the collective level, an environment or universuum which permits no outside intervention. According to Ellul, we have moved from a situation where technique was a strategic factor in society (The Technological Society), to the point where today it defines our entire milieu or system (The Technological System). See The Technological System, pp. 90, 199. Our second example is taken from his book Hope in Time of Abandonment. Here, when Ellul makes the bold claim that God is silent today and no longer speaking to his people, he does not deny that God is still speaking to certain, individual believers who have remained faithful to him. His point is that "it is from our history, our societies, our cultures, our sciences, and our politics that God is absent" (p. 72). For other statements on Ellul's distinction between the individual and the collective, see The Technological Society, p. xxviii, Boli-Bennett (pp. 181-184), Cérézuelle (pp. 167-169), and Temple's article in Research in Philosophy and Technology (p. 249).

[30] Ibid., p. 270. Ellul goes on to suggest, though, in this paragraph quoted, that despite this fact, there are grave consequences on the collective level of society if Christians do not exercise their individual liberty.

sense of fatality."[31]   Ellul proposes to show why this is not legitimate and how it came about. Today we face a "new kind of determinism"[32] that is qualitatively worse than at any point in history. Civilization, he contends, has become "absolutely totalitarian."[33]   This is not a biased value judgement but the clear teaching of all the social sciences. Social structures, heredity, public opinion, environment, group membership, education, and a host of other sociological determinants condition our lives in a variety of ways.[34] Van Hook correctly summarizes that "Ellul sees man as determined rather than as free; but he is determined not by some form of predestination, but by biological, psychological and sociological factors."[35]

Even man's best efforts at liberty and freedom go awry. Revolutionary movements intent on liberating people backfire into oppressive regimes. Vulgarized and domesticated, modern "revolutions" are, most often, anything but freeing. They are, says Ellul, typically and "unbearably oppressive."[36]   The French Revolution, which freed people from the absolutism of Louis XVI and the old regime, led to Robespierre, the Reign of Terror, and eventually to Napoleon. DeTocqueville was right: the clamor for equality overruled the quest for genuine liberty, and, in the end, hardly anything had changed.

-----

[31] Idem, _Autopsy_, p. 248.

[32] Idem, _Hope_, p. 7.   Temple, it seems to me, is wrong at this point, when she suggests that Ellul "does not say that our civilization is any worse than previous ones."   See her dissertation, p. 178.

[33] Idem, _POK_, p. 124.

[34] Idem, _The Ethics of Freedom_, pp. 31-37.   According to Ellul, "if we follow what the social sciences teach us today, we have to agree that as experience and knowledge increase the list of spheres of human determinism increases also" (p. 33).   This is not a metaphysical value judgement but the conclusion of "detailed investigations, as scientific as they can possibly be" (p. 31).

[35] Jay M. Van Hook, "The Politics of Man, the Politics of God, and the Politics of Freedom," in _JE:IE_, p. 136.

[36] This is a major theme of his work, _Autopsy of Revolution_. See, for example, pages 173, and, especially, 248-250.

Ellul observes what he calls "the perversity of history in bringing about the exact opposite of what we were fighting for."[37] The revolution of 1917 led to bloody dictatorships, while the revolution of 1933 "buried itself in the concentration camps."[38] Mankind's efforts at freedom seem to produce the exact opposite, oppression and necessity, so that there is a paradoxical reversal or what Ellul calls "the transmutation of the original intention into its opposite."[39]

Ellul's general prognosis, then, is that humankind is closed in, confined, and impotent. Humanity's situation is "fundamentally hopeless,"[40] and without the prospect of any possible solution.[41] He detects "a rising tide of disaster" which indicates that we are "approaching the end."[42] Necessity and determinism have swallowed up human freedom: "When we refer to the determinations which affect man, this totality forces us to consider that man lives in a universe of necessity...I have to accept the fact that there are necessities which we cannot escape."[43] From this general overview of Ellul's prognosis, we turn now to a particular analysis of how these deterministic forces rob man of his freedom. We shall illustrate this by a sequel of fatalities in the two spheres of the church and society at large.

C. Necessity: The First Pole of the Dialectic

1. General Definition

Ellul writes about necessity from both the sociological and

---

[37]Ellul, Living Faith, p. 215.

[38]Idem, Hope, p. 19.

[39]Ibid., p. 20. Compare his similar evaluation in Betrayal, p. 148.

[40]Ibid., p. vii. The entire part I of this book is given to documenting and illustrating this thesis, that man today has "no hope, no meaning, no way out, no history" (p. vii).

[41]Idem, POOA, p. 70. Note, however, Ellul's caveat on p. 74 of this book.

[42]Idem. Living Faith, p. 201. See the entire part III of this book, where Ellul tries to show in what sense this is true.

[43]Idem, The Ethics of Freedom, pp. 37-38.

the theological perspectives. To understand him correctly, we must address ourselves to both levels. His theological perspective, which we shall examine first, requires us to decipher his views on creation, before and after the Fall.

Before the Fall as recorded in Genesis 3, God's creation, and our relation to it and to God, were characterized by love, freedom, and spontaneity. In short, everything was perfect and complete. Mankind added nothing at all to God's creation; he served no demiurgic function. There was no "work" or "technique" in this perfect creation, according to Ellul:

> It was a creation which had been made for the love and joy of God. It was the very place of freedom, for nothing could be the expression of God except the freedom of his creation. Nothing could have responded to God except the spontaneous free gift. Nothing could have loved God except the free play of the creature turned toward his Creator...There cannot be any necessity in that creation because God is not subject to necessity.[44]

This perfect creation needed no cultivation, for example, because it spontaneously gave to man what he needed. Ellul writes that the relationship of the three persons of the Trinity illustrates man's pre-Fall relationship to God and creation: "The relationship within creation...was an immediate relationship of love and knowledge...[Adam spoke to God] face to face." [45] Based on the freedom of God himself, mankind in all his relationships was free from necessity. Creation, then, was characterized by the total absence of necessity. All this changed, however, with the Fall.

Ellul cannot agree with those who, in any way, would minimize the significance of the Fall. He describes himself as holding to what he calls "the most traditional interpretation of the event."[46] Loss of communion with God was one result of

---

[44]Idem, To Will and To Do, pp. 59-60.

[45]Idem, "Technique and the Opening Chapters of Genesis," in Carl Mitcham and Jim Grote, eds. Theology and Technology: Essays in Christian Analysis and Exegesis (New York: University Press of America, 1984), p. 129. Compare Ellul's other article in this book on a similar subject, "The Relationship Between Man and Creation in the Bible" (pp. 139-155).

[46]Idem, To Will and To Do, pp. 59-60.

the Fall, but, more broadly, Ellul describes the Fall as bringing about a transition from an order of freedom to an order of necessity. Whereas Adam was formerly free, communing with God spontaneously and in love, now he knows, experiences, and is subject to necessity.[47] His relations used to be free, spontaneous, and immediate. Now they are subject to necessity and require intermediaries. The perfect unity of the creation, its spontaneity, love and freedom, is now shattered. Adam hides from God, accuses his wife of their tragedy, must toil with a now unwieldly nature, and so on. For the first time, according to Ellul, technique now enters and serves in a mediating function, being "a product of necessity and not of human freedom."[48] In sum, then, Ellul maintains that

> Adam has now been placed in a _truly_ new situation. He knows necessity, a few aspects of which have been recalled. Previously, Adam had lived in freedom, and his work was freedom, play, child-like. He was free to be himself in front of his Creator who was his Father. He was free from all constraint, all obligation. He knew only this freedom, with its complement of respect for the will of God, respect within a free love and a free dialogue. There was no law, but an order--the very order of the freedom of God. From the moment when Adam separated himself from God, when his freedom was no longer love but the choice between two possibilities, from that moment Adam moved from the realm of freedom into the realm of necessity.[49]

In one sense, Ellul suggests that the creation needs these constraints of necessity to preserve it. Without the new order of necessity, "creation would disappear," for man's freedom now

---

[47] Idem, "Technique and the Opening Chapters of Genesis," p. 134.

[48] Ibid., p. 135.

[49] Ibid., p. 134. Cf. Augustine's _non posse non peccare_. For Ellul's ideas on work and vocation, see his article, "Work and Calling," trans. James S. Albritton, _Katallagete: Be Reconciled_, vol. 4, nos. 3-4 (Fall-Winter): 8-16. As Hanks observes in her annotation for this heading in her bibliography, for Ellul, "Work should not be identified with the Christian vocation or calling, although the Christian calling should find expression in some specific action. In the technical world this action will be a calling into question of the apparent social order" (_Jacques Ellul: A Comprehensive Bibliography_, p. 48).

operates without the guiding influence of filial love, but instead with fear, shame, doubt and the like, and hence, it can only be destructive.[50] Thus, necessity helps to preserve the world. Morality, for example, suggests Ellul, is of the order of necessity. There was no need for it in the pre-Fall order of freedom. Yet even though it issues forth from the order of necessity, morality is not without value. No society can live without moral values or some type of ethics. Ellul makes this same point, but about civil law, in his book The Theological Foundation of Law. Yet, despite this positive, preserving function of necessity, "the break with God leads to a slavery which expresses itself in the order of necessity."[51] Elsewhere we read that, "Brought about by the Fall, necessity is introduced into the world. Determinism, mechanism of history, scientific law, destiny, ananke, whatever name is used to cover it up, necessity is always the same."[52]

Thus, necessity has its origin in the Fall. In general we can say that it points to a loss of freedom and spontaneous communion with God, and the transition from immediate relationships with others and creation to mediated relationships with the same. A theological consequence, then, is that man is no longer able not to sin. Indeed, "Scripture certainly tells us that man is rigorously determined by his sinful condition." [53] In order to define further what Ellul means by this order of necessity, we can move on to his analysis of it on the sociological level, keeping in mind that all forms of sociological necessity have their roots or origin in the basic cleavage of the Fall. Three examples help to illustrate this.

First, and briefly, Ellul argues that it is a simple social scientific fact that people are conditioned by and subject to any number of what we might call "necessities"--things such as environment, family, social allegiances, jobs, biological needs, and so on. This is obvious, but not unimportant. "We are all given over to fate, to necessity. We are conditioned, whether biologically, culturally, socially, economically or by political dictatorship."[54] It is a "facile evasion" to deny or to

---

[50] Idem, To Will and To Do, pp. 60-61.

[51] Ibid., p. 280.

[52] Ibid., p. 59.

[53] Idem, The Ethics of Freedom, p. 47.

[54] Idem, "How I Discovered Hope," The Other Side (March 1980): 29.

downplay these scientific findings of sociology, psychology, economics, political science, and so on.[55]

A second example on the sociological level is social or political revolution. Nothing would seem to exemplify better man's freedom, his spirit for and ability to instigate change, than political revolutions. As Ellul shows, there have been revolutions galore in modern history.[56] On the surface level, the level of superficial investigation mentioned above, these many revolutions seem to have altered society radically. Nothing could be further from the truth, Ellul contends. True revolution is dead and gone, and Ellul provides us with its "autopsy." The supposed change brought about by past revolutions is only formal and not material, apparent and not real.[57] Society "goes on building and organizing itself with terrible implacability."[58] Not change or ferment but rigidity characterizes our society.

Thus, we might define necessity as cultural sclerosis or inertia, crystallization of the social body, wholesale conformity, adaptation, paralysis, entropy, obligation, static uniformity, or assimilation. Not an abundance, but a total lack of truly revolutionary ferment plagues society: "I say on the contrary that there is not enough chaos."[59] As we shall see, one function of Christian freedom is to introduce points of "chaos" or "tension" into this social realm of necessity, implacability, and impermeability. Freedom must break the otherwise closed circle of necessity.

Contemporary revolutions are, in reality, the exact opposite of what they propose to be. According to Ellul, they

---

[55] Idem, The Ethics of Freedom, p. 36.

[56] Idem, Autopsy, pp. vii-viii, footnote #1. This passage cited, by the way, it an excellent example of the breadth and depth of Ellul's mastery of human history.

[57] Ellul makes this point in several places. For several examples, see his articles "Problems of Sociological Method," Social Research 43, no. 1 (Spring 1976): 13; "Social Change," in Carl F.H. Henry, ed., Baker's Dictionary of Christian Ethics (Grand Rapids: Baker Book House, 1973), pp. 629-632; and "Between Chaos and Paralysis."

[58] Ellul, "Between Chaos and Paralysis," p. 747.

[59] Ibid.

have become "unbearably oppressive."[60] True revolution, on the other hand, runs "against the predictable course of history," against that necessity which Ellul labels "the negation of freedom."[61] As the opposite of necessity, it would introduce into society such characteristics as mobility, fluidity, uncertainty, variation, and creativity.

Our third example of necessity on the sociological level is Ellul's discussion of violence. It is a helpful example, too, for, in the end, he overlaps and combines it with the theological perspective of the effects of the Fall. In his book on this subject, Ellul devotes an entire section of one chapter to "Violence as Necessity."[62] Here we can only note some of his main emphases.

Violence can take many forms besides its physical expression. There can be the political violence of a dictatorship, the economic violence of class divisions brought about by free competition, or psychological violence in any number of ways. At any rate, widespread social violence is of the order of necessity in the sense that people or groups follow what Ellul calls "the given trends...these inescapable compulsions."[63] That is, they fail to exercise any moral independence and instead follow the prevailing herd instinct, the general rule or course of events. By doing so, a person shows "that he is acting on the animal level and obeying a necessity; that he is not free."[64]

To conclude this section on the theological and sociological perspectives of Ellul's definition of necessity, we can recall a rather long passage from his book <u>Violence</u>, a passage which combines the two levels. I quote at length so as to let Ellul speak for himself and because it provides a good summary of his definition, especially vis-à-vis the opposing order of freedom.

> [T]o have true freedom is to escape necessity or, rather, to be free to struggle against necessity... For the order of necessity is the order of separation

---

[60] Idem, <u>Autopsy</u>, p. 173.

[61] Ibid., pp. 249-250.

[62] See <u>Violence</u>, Chapter 3, pp. 84-93.

[63] Ellul, <u>Violence</u>, p. 91.

[64] Ibid., p. 92.

from God. Adam, created by God and in communion with
God, is free; he is not subject to any kind of necessity...Adam knows nothing of necessity, obligation,
inevitability...Necessity appears when Adam breaks
his relation with God. Then he becomes subject to an
order of obligation, the order of toil, hunger,
passions, struggles against nature, etc., from which
there is no appeal. At that moment necessity becomes
part of the order of nature... Necessity is definable
as what man does because he cannot do otherwise. But
when God reveals himself, necessity ceases to be
destiny or even inevitability...[T]his freedom is
fully accomplished by and through Jesus Christ...[W]e
understand that the whole of Christ's work is a work
of liberation...[and hence] the role of the Christian
in society, in the midst of men, is to shatter
fatalities and necessities.[65]

2. Particular Illustrations

If our thesis is accurate that the freedom/necessity
dialectic is the hermeneutical key to Ellul's entire corpus,
then we would expect some evidence that such is the case. In
this section we propose to do just that, to illustrate how in
the two spheres of the church and society, the same recurring
problem of necessity surfaces. We begin with the church.

If any institution or group of people has the power to
exercise freedom within the order of necessity, it is the
church. That is obvious, from Ellul's perspective. Yet despite
all its claims to the contrary, the church has historically been
the enemy of freedom and an agent of necessity, oppression and

---

[65]Ibid., pp. 127-129. As odd as it may seem, the best
comparable definition of "necessity" in Ellul's sense of the
term, which I have been able to find, is in Charles Dickens' A
Christmas Carol. Scrooge, having just witnessed his vision of
the Ghost of Christmas Future, inquires, "Are these [i.e., his
vision] the shadows of things that Will Be, or are they shadows
of things that May be, only? Men's courses will foreshadow
certain ends, to which, if preserved in, they must lead...But if
the courses be departed from, the ends will change. Say it is
thus with what you show me!" See "A Christmas Carol," in A
Charles Dickens Christmas (New York: Oxford University Press,
1976), pp. 88-90. Kenneth Konyndyk also proffers one of the
best definitions of Ellul's idea of necessity I have seen, in
his article, "Violence," in JE:IE (pp. 260 ff.).

intolerance. It professes to liberate people, but too often it has fettered and crushed them. One need but recall such glaring examples as the Crusades or the Inquisition to illustrate this. Too often the church has proffered to her own a mere "false presence of the kingdom," to use the title of one of Ellul's works. Much of Ellul's corpus, then, is a stern critique of this ecclesiastical betrayal, and an effort, like Kierkegaard's, to reintroduce authentic Christianity into Christendom. Although Christianity itself should be "subversive," calling into question the cultural status quo, Ellul's point is that, instead, the church itself has been subverted.[66] This is a major thesis of his recent work La Subversion du christianisme.

When Ellul writes about the church, we must remember that this critique is not carried out in a spirit of condemnation, superiority, or aloofness.[67] The situation is more like that of a lovers' quarrel. Ellul is passionately devoted to the church, and loves it dearly. For 21 years he served on the National Council of the Reformed Church, the ruling body of that denomination. He claims that his efforts to reform the church's structure "failed totally,"[68] while his attempts to revitalize its theological education met with only limited success.[69] Even the church of unskilled laborers which he helped to nurture as their pastor grew from ten people to over fifty families, only to succumb to the pressures of institutionalization. Ellul's experience in the church has not been a "happy" one and for this reason it is not hard to appreciate his constructive criticism of it. Of the many examples we could choose to illustrate the church's complicity in the order of necessity, we shall use two pairs of opposing terms.

The first antithesis is between revelation and religion, a major theme in his writings and one which follows closely Barth's treatment of the same matter. One of the greatest dangers facing the church is "that Christianity in this society be readapted as religion... [and] that the church seek at any

---

[66]David Gill, in his book review of La Subversion du christianisme, in Fides et Historia, cited previously.

[67]See, for example, FPOK, pp. 4-5.

[68]Ellul, ISOS, p. 88.

[69]Ibid., chapter 8. Ellul also recounts some of his church experiences in his article "Mirror of These Ten Years," trans. Cecelia Gaul Kings Christian Century 87 (February 19, 1970): 200-204.

price to adapt itself to culture."[70] It is sad but true that all too often the church "acts purely and simply as a sociological body" without any distinctives which one could say are truly Christian.[71] To the extent that Christianity is merely a human phenomenon, it is opposed to revelation and has lapsed into religion. It has been subverted.

Religion, he writes, is the product of our own fears, anxieties and efforts whereby we create God in our own image. As such, religion belongs to the order of necessity, and Ellul would subscribe wholeheartedly to its critique by Feuerbach and Marx. Religion is the opposite of freedom, "an expression of ineluctable forces" which enslaves people. Such is the verdict of Monos in Living Faith.[72] This sociological conformity entails the loss of the church's true distinctives so that the typical church member lives thinks, works, and reacts like everyone else.[73] The "crushing dominance of the bureaucratic machine,"[74] epitomized, according to Ellul, by the World Council of Churches,[75] saps the church of its dynamic liberty

---

[70]Idem, "Social Change," in Baker's Dictionary of Christian Ethics, p. 631. One of the most unfortunate examples of this, according to Ellul, is the church's wholesale and indiscriminate acceptance of liberation theologies. His entire book FPOK is directed to this problem.

[71]Idem, FPOK, pp. 73ff. Ellul does not imagine, of course, that the church can avoid institutionalization, or that it is not a sociological group. His criticism is that the church is nothing more than this.

[72]Idem, Living Faith, p. 27. Una, the other character in the dialogue, takes the opposite position. According to Una, "belief is where our freedom of choice and hence our responsibility is actualized...This state of freedom always comes from belief" (pp. 53, 88). See the entire part II for Ellul's distinctions between belief and faith, religion and revelation.

[73]Idem, FPOK, p. 46.

[74]Idem, Hope, p. 137.

[75]See his article, "Mirror of These Ten Years," where Ellul discusses the WCC. According to Ellul, "through experience, I had reached the conviction that the Council was on the way to becoming a bureaucratic system, an enormous machine that, the larger it grew, the more it conformed to sociological laws of organization, rather than obeying promptings of the Holy Spirit" (p. 202).

and instead adopts a stance of static conformism. In such a condition, the church forfeits its uniqueness as a _sui generis_ body in favor of "conformity to the average opinion."[76] By lapsing into religion or Christendom, the church reflects an enslavement to necessity and the cultural status quo and, consequently, its denial of freedom.

The second antithesis which illustrates the church's opposition to liberty and participation in necessity is that between morality and ethics. We have already noted above that morality is of the order of the Fall, tragic destiny and necessity, even if it does serve a useful function in the present age. Morality involves rules, restraints, duties and obligations. This manmade churchly morality "is never an act of freedom."[77] It requires no personal decision, individual virtues, or critical reflection, for, almost without exception, it represents mere habitual conformity to social mores.[78]

True ethics, on the other hand, the "ethics of freedom," require a fight of faith, a style of life, a living attitude, and, above all, a relation to Jesus Christ. It engenders a freedom which is alive, absolute, and unrestricted, enabling one to do away with external constraints.[79] The church's propagation of a worldly morality in place of a true christian ethic is but a particular example of the general trend whereby it conforms to religion and forfeits freedom rather than listens to revelation and combats the order of necessity.

Thus, while the church ought to be the standard bearer of freedom, it all too often illustrates the opposite:

Ought to be! Alas, time and again for almost 2,000 years the churches have obstinately done exactly the opposite of this 'ought'--concealing the gravity of

---

[76] Ellul, _Hope_, p. 151.

[77] Idem, _To Will and To Do_, p. 63.

[78] Ellul gives the illustration somewhere that, for example, poorer Christians most often preach about such things as social justice, while wealthier Christians, on the other hand, extol the virtues of individualism, stewardship, freedom, and so on. Each group, therefore, shows little creativity and instead reflects its own group values.

[79] Ellul, _The Ethics of Freedom_, p. 186.

75

the problems, evading the issues, opposing all revolutionary tendencies, holding to the forces of order,
conservativism, and traditional morality and adapting
themselves to these...[Too often] Christians are of
all men the most conformist, the most compliant, the
most bound by habit, the least free.[80]

Such is our first of two foci, the sphere of the church, in
which we see that the primary battle is between the two opposing
orders of freedom and necessity. We now turn from the sphere of
the church to society at large, directing our attention to the
three subjects to which Ellul has devoted extended study,
technique, propaganda, and politics. Here, too, we find that
the gist of Ellul's critique revolves around his belief that the
collective forces of necessity have usurped individual liberty.

It is a facile commonplace of our society to imagine that
modern man has "come of age," that he is, above all else,
rational, scientific and free.[81] Precisely the opposite is
true, suggests Ellul. Never has humankind been so uncritical
and gullible, so intensely religious and irrational. Our age is
certainly post-Christian, but it is hardly "secular." Never
have people been so willing to worship and to enslave themselves
to the "new demons" of our society which constitute a new realm
of the sacred.[82] This is most graphically illustrated by the
technical phenomenon which, as a desacralizing agent, has itself
been sacralized and worshipped. Our purpose here is not to
examine in depth the three phenomena of technique, propaganda,
and politics, something that has already been done well by
others many times. Rather, our goal is to show that these three
things are properly understood only when they are considered in
light of the greater context of the dialectic between freedom
and necessity.

Technique, writes Ellul, represents a new form of determinism, "the most dangerous form of determinism" in our modern
society.[83] His stated purpose in The Technological Society is
to "arouse the reader to an awareness of the technical

---

[80] Idem, "Between Chaos and Paralysis," p. 750.

[81] Idem, A Critique of the New Commonplaces, pp. 67-81.

[82] Idem, The New Demons, trans. C. Edward Hopkin (New
York: Seabury, 1975), p. 148.

[83] Idem, The Technological Society, p. xxxiii.

76

necessity."[84]   More   than   anything,   it   is   necessity   which
characterizes the technical phenomenon, for technique has become
the   primary   determinant   of our society.   As we noted above, if
Marx were alive today,   says   Ellul,   he   would   choose   it,   not
capital,   as   the   constituent element by which to understand and
interpret culture.[85]

We   have   already   observed   that   Ellul's   problem   with
technique   is   not that it is perverse, innately evil, or lacking
any good qualities.   His attitude is not that we should avoid   it
at   all   costs.   He   has   never   said   this.   According to him,
technical progress is "neither exclusively positive   nor   totally
negative...[and]   I   would   certainly never wish to maintain that
technology was to be deplored."[86]   In   his   words,   the   results
of   technique are "ambivalent."   Technique has obviously provided
man   with   many   new   "freedoms,"   such   as   freedoms   from   the
restrictions   of   time   and   space via travel and communications.
If   Ellul   has   written   precious   little   on   the   benefits   of
technique,   it   is   because   they   are so obvious that they hardly
need to be mentioned.

Why,   then,   is Ellul so outspokenly   critical   of   technique?
The   root   problem,   I   suggest,   is the problem of necessity and
freedom:

When I say   that   I   'despise   technology,'   I   should
perhaps   explain.   It   is   not technology per se, but
the   authoritarian power that   the   'technocrats'   seek
to   exercise,   as   well   as   the   fact that technology

---

[84] Ibid.   Compare   page   116   of this same book, where Ellul
writes: "In this description [of technique]   we   have   constantly
encountered   the   term   necessity;   it   is   necessity   which
characterizes   the   technical   universe.   Everything   must
accommodate   itself   to   it   with   mathematical   certainty."   The
emphasis is his own.

[85] Idem, ISOS, pp. 175-176.

[86] Idem, "The Technological   Revolution   and   Its   Moral   and
Political   Consequences,"   in   Johannes   Metz,   ed.,   The Evolving
World and Theology (New York: Paulist   Press,   1967),   pp.   100,
107.   I could multiply references like this, for, as we noted in
Chapter One, this is a charge Ellul   continually   faces   and   one
which   he   never tires of refuting.   For a few sample refutations
of the charge that technique is bad see Hope, pp.   237-238;   POK,
pp.   24, 87; POOA, 70, 82, 108; and Autopsy, p. 275.

determines our lives without our being able to intervene or, as yet, to control it.[87]

That is, the net effect of the overall technical phenomenon as a whole and on the collective level produces what he calls "an operational totalitarianism."[88] In another article Ellul begins by "disembarassing" his readers of four "fake problems" (one of which is to imagine that technique is innately bad). He then proceeds to discuss the "real problem,"[89] which is the question of whether people will be enslaved to technique and its necessities, or whether they can remain masters, subjects in control and not objects under control. An extensive quote from this article is revealing:

> Technique can never engender freedom...The problem is deeper--the operation of Technique is the contrary of freedom, an operation of determinism and necessity. Technique is an ensemble of rational and efficient practices, a collection of orders, schemas, and mechanisms. All of this expresses very well a necessary order and a determinate process, but one into which freedom, unorthodoxy and the sphere of the gratuitous and spontaneous cannot penetrate...The more technical activities increase in society, the more human autonomy and initiative diminish. The more the human being comes to exist in a world of everincreasing demands, the more he loses any possibility of free choice and individuality in actions...But where freedom is excluded in this way, an authentic civilization has little chance.[90]

The issue at stake, then, is a struggle between the forces of freedom and necessity, and not the superficial suggestion that technique is bad.

A brief overview of Ellul's characterology of technique further illustrates the importance of the freedom/necessity dialectic as a hermeneutical key to his thought. In The Technological Society we read that "technique is nothing more

---

[87] Idem, POOA, p. 26.

[88] Idem, "Conformism and the Rationale of Technique," p. 90.

[89] Idem, "The Technological Order," p. 88.

[90] Ibid., pp. 90-91.

than means and the ensemble of means."[91] Ellul argues in another book that technical means have effaced all ends, the end result being the individual's loss of freedom: "The irremedial triumph of means takes away all liberty from man."[92]

In his two massive works on technique, The Technological Society and The Technological System, Ellul characterizes technique by seven traits, each of which demonstrates, from a slightly different angle, that the problem involves a loss of freedom and enslavement to necessity. (1) Technique is self-directing; it follows its own rules and endures no outside interference or personal choice. This is the characteristic of automatism which, in effect, takes away from man the freedom of choice in the realm of technical matters.[93] (2) Technique is also self-augmenting, meaning that one technique gives rise to another with a progression that is geometric and irreversible. (3) Technique forms a whole, an impenetrable system, or enclosed milieu (monism). It comprises a single essence which, despite extremely diverse appearances in the particulars, has a singular nature. (4) Closely akin to this is the unity of technique. All the various forms of technique are linked together so that it is impossible to isolate any one phenomenon by itself. The multiple techniques, therefore, are interdependent. Television, for example, requires a host of different techniques, none of which, however, can be separated. Those might include such things as advertising, federal regulations, communications, economics, and so on. (5) Technique has now become universal, both geographically and qualitatively, so that it "cannot be otherwise than totalitarian...Everything must be subordinated to it. Technique can leave nothing untouched...Everything is its concern."[94] (6) Technique is also autonomous, meaning it tolerates no feedback or outside value judgements. In fact, technique creates its own set of new values such as speed, efficiency, and rationality, none of which are, practically speaking, subject to questioning. Who today, for example, would deny the maxim that "faster is better"? (7) Finally, Ellul refers to the characteristic of totalization. That is, our

---

[91] Idem, The Technological Society, p. 19.

[92] Idem, POK, p. 77. Ellul devotes an entire chapter of this book to "The End and the Means" (pp. 61-95). Compare his discussion in A Critique of the New Commonplaces (pp. 294-303) where he attempts to refute the axiom that "the end justifies the means."

[93] Idem, The Technological Society, p. 84.

[94] Ibid., p. 125.

concern with technique does not have to do with any of its constituent parts but with the overall whole. One must think of technique in terms of a total system. To do this, "the first condition is to regard it as a whole."[95] Technique, according to Ellul, is "an all-inclusive ensemble, in which what counts is not so much each of its parts as the system of relations and connections between them."[96]

The paradox of all this is that most people see technology as the great liberator of mankind.[97] It seems to offer us unlimited power to control our lives and to order our destinies. In typical fashion, Ellul contends that precisely the opposite is true. Technique enslaves people. It proffers them the mere illusion of freedom through its near-infinite arsenal of means. Through the human techniques of amusement, to take just one of Ellul's examples, technicians make tolerable what should naturally remain intolerable. They "render unnoticeable the disadvantages that other techniques have created," giving rise to the paradox that "the application of technique designed to liberate men should end in subjecting them the more harshly to it."[98] We should not think, however, that this technological system or environment is now or ever will be a society of gloom, despair, agony or the like. As John Wilkinson put it so well in his translator's introduction to The Technological Society, "The denizen of the technological state of the future will have everything his heart ever desired, except, of course, his freedom."[99]

---

[95] Idem, The Technological System, p. 90.

[96] Ibid., p. 199.

[97] Ellul mentions Alvin Toffler as one example of the technical partisan who "declares that technological society opens the way to greater liberty" (The Technological System, p. 319). Miller briefly mentions the "Attitudes of Christian Theologians Toward Technology" in Chapter II of his dissertation. According to him, those who see technology as a negative factor include Nicholas Berdyaev, Gabriel Marcel, Emil Brunner, Paul Tillich, and Romano Guardini (p. 24). Those who see it as a positive factor include Jean Danielou, Norris Clark, Thomas Neil, Teilhard de Chardin, Walter Ong, and Myron Bloy (p. 27).

[98] Ellul, The Technological Society, pp. 412-413.

[99] John Wilkinson, "The Translator's Introduction," in The Technological Society, p. xvii.

Propaganda is the "Siamese twin" of technique.[100] It too is both an enemy of freedom (personally and politically) and an "inescapable necessity" in our society.[101] Governments, for example, have no choice but to use it, and individuals literally need it. Among its many purposes, propaganda has as its goal the production of a certain general conception of society or way of life which becomes an indisputable criterion of value (such as "the American Way of Life"). Everything, then, which conforms to this world view is "good," and anything which takes exception to it is "bad." Propaganda's link with technique is easily seen, for "in the midst of increasing mechanization and technological organization, propaganda is simply the means to prevent these things from being felt as too oppressive and to persuade men to submit with good grace."[102] It provides the consummate means for the illusion of freedom whereby people do by necessity what they think they do by personal choice or freedom. Propaganda, Ellul says, destroys one's personality and freedom.[103]

Instead of defining propaganda,[104] we shall look briefly at three of its characteristics, each of which demonstrates how it is a deterministic factor which threatens individual freedom. First, propaganda is total. It utilizes all available means (radio, T.V., posters, meetings, and so on) in a variety of combinations. Its goal is to influence the total person,

---

[100]Konrad Kellen, in the "Introduction" to Propaganda: The Formation of Men's Attitudes, trans. Konrad Kellen and John Lerner (New York: Knopf, 1965), p.v.

[101]Ellul, Propaganda, p. xv. See his entire chapter 3 of this book, entitled "The Necessity of Propaganda."

[102]Ibid., p. xviii.

[103]Ibid., p. 137.

[104]Ellul's definition of propaganda is on page 61 of his book: "Propaganda is a set of methods employed by an organized group that wants to bring about the active or passive participation in its actions of a mass of individuals, psychologically unified through psychological manipulations and incorporated in an organization." Just as with technique, Ellul is interested in the phenomenon as a whole and on the collective level. This permits him to exclude certain types of propaganda and to make the claim that all propaganda is the same, no matter what its origin. That is, the content of propaganda might differ, but not its characteristics or its subsequent effects on those who are under its influence. The net effect, then, of propaganda, say, from Russia and the U.S., is essentially the same.

including his feelings, ideas, will, needs, and actions.
Propaganda tolerates no independent thought, critique, or
freedom of opinion and in that sense it is thoroughly totalitarian.[105] Next, propaganda is continuous and lasting. It
fills all our days and moments, and is sustained for long
durations of time. This, says Ellul, renders personal
resistance and/or critical reflection almost impossible. Third,
propaganda is aimed not only at orthodoxy but at orthopraxy. It
intends to modify not only our ideas but our actions. This
makes group integration all the more effective and the long term
effects of propaganda enduring. Like the other two traits, the
goal of orthopraxy short-circuits critical analysis by
separating our thoughts from our actions.

As an example of the antithesis between freedom and
necessity as it concerns propaganda, let us briefly observe its
effects on democracy.[106] As Fasching observes, "it has become
a commonplace to observe that politics is the arena of human
freedom, the arena in which human beings choose their destiny
and exercise control over their lives."[107] What is the effect
of propaganda on democracy, the supposed epitome of political
freedom? First, a democracy needs propaganda, for it is based
on the participation of an informed public opinion. Hence, a
democratic government must make and use propaganda. If it did
not, it could never shape public opinion for its own cause, and
thus it could never come to or remain in power. Furthermore,
democratic governments have no choice but to utilize propaganda, for all of the competing governments of the world use it.
To the degree that a democratic propagandist respects the
individual, he loses all the effectiveness of propaganda, for
propaganda abolishes the true democratic ideals of tolerance,
diversity, understanding of others, freedom of expression,
respect for the minority opinion, critical examination of your
own cherished beliefs, the absence of dogmatism, and so
on. [108] Group conformity, adaptation, and integration: these
are the true goals of propaganda which subvert individual
liberty.

The third element of our society to which Ellul has devoted
special attention, in addition to technique and propaganda, is

---

[105]Ellul, Propaganda, p. 16.

[106]See Propaganda, pages 232-257, where Ellul discusses
"Propaganda and Democracy."

[107]Fasching, The Thought of Jacques Ellul, p. 26.

[108]Ellul, Propaganda, pp. 250, 256.

politics and the state. In this realm, too, Ellul sees the primary threat to be the force of necessity. As with his involvements with the church, we should keep in mind that Ellul does not criticize politics as an ivory-towered intellectual but as one who has been actively involved in politics all of his adult life. It is from his personal experience of repeated frustrations and failures in the political realm that Ellul has developed what he confesses is a "mistrust and even hatred of political circles."[109]

Many people see the state as the primary agent of freedom. Ellul thinks just the opposite is the case, that the modern centralized state is one of the "surest destroyers of freedom."[110] He recognizes, of course, that the state has a legitimate role to play as, in Fasching's words, "simply the modest and useful administrator of the common patrimony."[111] Yet, in most circumstances, the state has gone far beyond this modest function until it constitutes "the chief danger known to man, whether from the material standpoint or from the spiritual standpoint."[112]

It constitutes the chief threat to personal freedom not because of its ideological bent (socialist, communist, or democratic), but because of its increasing centralization of

---

[109]Idem, ISOS, p. 56. Ellul's political involvements include the Popular Front of 1936, the Personalist movement, the Spanish revolution, the liberation of 1943-44, the Algerian war, environmental concerns, and a stint as the deputy mayor of Bordeaux. All of these, he writes, "formed an accumulation of ruined revolutionary possibilities. After this, I never believed anything could be changed by this route" (p. 56). Compare his similar statements in POOA, pages 23, and 71.

[110]Idem, Betrayal, p. 21. Robert Nisbet recognizes this point about Ellul in JE:IE, p. viii.

[111]Fasching, The Thought of Jacques Ellul, p. 155. See Ellul's The Ethics of Freedom, page 382, and The Theological Foundation of Law, pages 76-77. In the latter passage, Ellul recognizes the state as a divinely given institution.

[112]Ellul, The Ethics of Freedom, p. 396. In this passage, made some 30 years after the statement in footnote #111 about the state as a divinely given institution, Ellul changes his position on the idea that a state can claim to be instituted by God. We must keep in mind, however, that this apparent change would be congruent with his advocacy of a "double attitude" toward the state.

power and its complex web of bureaucracy which encroaches upon nearly every aspect of our lives. With typical hyperbole, Ellul claims that "every modern state is totalitarian," for the simple reason that "it recognizes no limit either factual or legal" to its sphere of authority.[113] Its vast arsenal of technical means (economic, juridical, military, investigative, communicative, informational and so on) invests the state with a nearly incontestable power. Ellul illustrates this by examining the state's role in commerce, planning, banking, organization, psychology, art, science, biology, sociology, and so on.[114] Although the state and all political power will be done away with in the New Jerusalem,[115] for the time being, its increased power and sphere of influence deprive people of their individual liberties.

Much the same is true when we turn from the state in particular to politics in general, which, Ellul says, represents "the supreme religion of this age,"[116] and the consummate illusion of personal freedom. He goes so far as to label politics the realm of the demonic: "Politics is the contemporary image of absolute evil. It is satanic, diabolical, the home base of the demonic...It is, strictly speaking, the source of all the evils that plague our time. And when I say that it is diabolical and satanic, I mean these adjectives literally." [117] Politization, the tendency to treat all problems politically, is the great evil of our age. "Politics first!" is yet another of society's commonplaces,[118] and woe to the

---

[113] Ibid.

[114] Idem, The Technological Society, p. 253. Ellul discusses the relation between technique and the state in Chapter IV of this book.

[115] See Apocalypse, pp. 187-189, 227-228. In a footnote #17 on page 279 of this book, Ellul diverges on this point from Barth, who claims that in the eschaton political power(s) will remain. Ellul could never tolerate such a position.

[116] Ellul, The New Demons, p. 167.

[117] Idem, Living Faith, pp. 234-235. Ellul makes a similar statement in FPOK, p. 112.

[118] Idem, A Critique of the New Commonplaces, pp. 92-109. The best example of this attitude I have found is in Bradley's thesis, pp. 53-54: According to Bradley, "The clearest statement of this approach [to politics] is probably Kwame (footnote continued on following page)

person who would deny or challenge this. The a-political person is dismissed as stupid; he is a heretic, a defeatist, and a bad citizen. Another example of "politization" concerns the realm of values. All values today are politicized. Truth, liberty, and justice, for example, have little meaning today apart from a political context. All life today is oriented toward politics. It has invaded everything and has been granted an unlimited sphere of power. Politics have attained true autonomy, permitting no outside criterion or values.[119]

Ellul focuses on three basic political illusions in his book The Political Illusion. These are the illusions of popular control (chapter IV), popular participation (chapter V), and popular problem solving (chapter VI), or the idea that politics can solve all problems. These three illusions coalesce to form a vicious cycle whereby people increasingly turn to politics for solutions to society's problems. This, in turn, leads to an unending growth both of the state's power and size, and to our dependence on it. Political "choices" can be made and voted on, of course, but Ellul says that these are only "pseudo-decisions" which have been "rigorously determined" from the outset.[120]

---

[118] (cont'd)...Nk'rumah's paraphrase of Matthew 6:33: 'Seek ye first the political kingdom and everything shall be added to you,' or another African leader who went on to say: 'For us, politics is the most important weapon with which to create the new type of man and society, the new and appropriate systems we want, and to build the strength needed to contend with older powers.'"

[119]Idem, The Political Illusion, trans. Konrad Kellen (New York: Knopf, 1967), pp. 68-95. Compare Ellul's similar comments vis-à-vis revolution in Autopsy, pp. 173ff.

[120]Ibid., p. 29. All of this does not mean that people should shun politics. That is neither possible, for politics imposes itself on us, nor desirable, for not to participate would only grant the state more unchecked power. According to Ellul, the "a-political attitude is in no sense a mark of freedom...The freedom to be uninterested, to turn aside, or to sleep is not Christian freedom. An a-political attitude in modern society is not an expression of Christian freedom but of fear and weakness" (The Ethics of Freedom, p. 375). Compare the entire section of this book which treats the theme of the Christian and politics (pp. 369-385). Ellul also addresses the error of the a-political attitude in POOA (p. 25), FPOK (p. 112), and in Subversion (Chapter 6, entitled "Political Perversion").

In conclusion, we can say that Ellul's primary critique of society in general, and his analysis of technique, propaganda, the state and politics in particular, has as its focus the freedom/necessity axis. Almost all of the problems which Ellul has with these phenomena have their source, either implicitly or explicitly, in this primary matrix. Darrell Fasching aptly summarizes for us the complex relation between technique, propaganda, and politics within this context of freedom and necessity:

> Ellul argues that politics is the point of convergence for technique and propaganda in this society. This is the point where they coalesce to create the illusion of freedom--the illusion of the control of technology through politics, by means of which technology seems to be an instrument of human freedom. [121]

At this point we can now move to a short summary of the first pole of the dialectic, necessity.

D. Conclusions on Necessity

Necessity and determinisms of all kinds threaten our lives. Our world, writes Ellul, has become "a collection of mechanisms of indescribable complexity--techniques, propaganda, state, administration, planning, ideology, urbanization, [and] social technology," over which we have less and less control, and all of which constrict and confine our personal lives.[122] The net result is that "man is less and less the master of his own life." [123] How can a person break this network of sociological and theological enslavement? What is our response to these "inescapable necessities?" According to Ellul, if we are to have any hope of combatting the world of necessity, there must be a force or aid which comes from outside this closed and impenetrable system. If there is not a transcendent reality which is "above" and "beyond" this world of determinisms, then we face "nothing but destiny."[124] Without such a reality "we

---

[121]Fasching, ibid., pp. 26-27. The emphasis is mine.

[122]Ellul, The Ethics of Freedom, p. 27.

[123]Ibid.

[124]Idem, Living Faith, p. 261.

can only let ourselves sink into despair."[125]

   If we were to focus on these aspects alone of Ellul's corpus, that is, the theological enslavement to sin as a result of the Fall, and the sociological determinants of technique, propaganda, the state, and politics which the Fall spawns, seen only from a sociological vantage point without the gospel perspective, we would be forced to charge him with rampant pessimism. But his "pessimism" is only on the sociological level, the level of necessity. In his own words, "My purely sociological and historical intellectual approach had led me into a blind alley. There was nothing to say to a person of my society beyond a stoic exhortation to keep going...This concrete situation was fundamentally hopeless."[126] But this would be to neglect the other pole of Ellul's dialectic, the counterpoint of freedom. According to him, there is a transcendent reality which can pierce the otherwise closed system of necessity and reintroduce a measure of authentic freedom. It is God, the God who reveals himself primarily as the liberator and who alone is incapable of being absorbed by the world.[127] Ellul's "pessimism" is only about man, not about God. This God, who has revealed himself in the person of Jesus Christ, proffers to all an authentic liberation which successfully counters the realm of necessity. This brings us to the other point of our hermeneutical key to Ellul's dialectic, the pole of freedom.

---

[125] Idem, ISOS, pp. 206-207.

[126] Idem, Hope, p. vii.

[127] Idem, The Ethics of Freedom, p. 51. Ellul makes the same point in POOA, pages 101-103. There, he writes, "Thus we meet this transcendent, whose sole action is an action of liberating us, a liberation which is always begun anew. This liberation can be guaranteed and certain only if God is this transcendent" (p. 103). The emphasis is Ellul's.

CHAPTER FOUR

THE DIALECTIC OF FREEDOM AND NECESSITY AS THE
HERMENEUTICAL KEY TO ELLUL'S THEOLOGICAL METHOD
PART TWO: FREEDOM AS THE POSITIVE POLE OF THE DIALECTIC

It is for freedom that Christ has set us free. Stand firm,
then, and do not let yourselves be burdened again by a yoke of
slavery.   Galatians 5:1

Where the Spirit of the Lord is there is liberty.
                                        2 Corinthians 3:16

A. Introduction

1. Review

The triumph of necessity and the loss of personal freedom
constitute the principal danger and chief characteristic of our
society, according to Ellul. This was the basic conclusion of
our last chapter.[1] The genesis or origin of the alienation
which expresses itself in necessity is theological in nature,
seen in Ellul's affirmation of the traditional doctrine of the
Fall and original sin. Humans are enslaved to sin, and "this
slavery includes, embraces all the others, [and] explains all
the others."[2] In other words, the reality of theological
enslavement to sin results in all manner of sociological determinisms. Ellul resolutely denies any metaphysical notion of
necessity. For him, necessity or determinism does not mean an
ineluctable destiny, deterministic causality or mechanistic
determinisms which come upon people no matter what. Rather, he
has in mind political slavery, economic alienation, sociological
conformity, enslavement to the passions, and so on, all of which

---

[1] Ellul, ISOS, p. 198.

[2] Idem, "Le Sens de la liberté chez St. Paul," Foi et Vie
61, no. 3 (May-June 1962):4. Hereafter referred to as "Le
Sens." This was one of Ellul's earliest exegetical studies, and
was first published in [Paulus-Hellas-Oikumene: An Ecumenical
Symposium (Athens: L'Association Chrétienne d'Etudiants de
Grèce, 1951)]. Much of it is incorporated into The Ethics of
Freedom.

"are only forms, expressions or aspects of this essential cleavage which is that of sin."[3]

Ellul elucidates some of these points in one of his recent articles, "L'Antidestin," which we shall use as a brief review of the last chapter and transition to our present chapter. On the one hand, people have always resisted any notion of metaphysical causality and have at least acted as if they were free. We struggle against and shape our natural environment, express ourselves in art, and so on. On the other hand, Ellul contends, all societies have expressed and struggled against some "sense of destiny, of the insurmountable, of the irreversible."[4] Whether this takes the form of the Greek myths and tragedies about "inexorable fate," the Romans' obsession with Chronos, Aztec fear of "the inevitable end," Hinduism's quest for total detachment and Nirvana, or what Ellul calls the "it is written" of Islam, the result is all the same: "the domination of destiny."[5]

We should not imagine that these examples represent the puerile fears of ancient civilizations, and that modern man "come of age" is immune from them. No, we discover precisely the same thing in our modern world, "the affirmation, more and more massive, of destiny in the form of determinism."[6] Only the forms have changed and are more subtle. Ellul uses the examples of 19th-century causal laws pertaining to science and history, or the 20th-century threat of "a doubly mechanistic determinism" which suggests that everything is determined by one's chromosones (anatomy is destiny) or by one's cultural inheritance.[7]

---

[3] Ibid. Compare The Ethics of Freedom, p. 76: "We have been at some pains not to describe alienation as fate, that is, as a universal and irremedial power which man can do nothing about, in which he does not participate, and which strictly conditions the totality of human life without any possibility of resistance or rejection. This is not our point."

[4] Idem, "L'Antidestin," Foi et Vie 84 (January 1985):114. In a remarkable way this article confirms the original thesis of the present book, that the dialectic of freedom and necessity is the key to Ellul's thought.

[5] Ibid., p. 116.

[6] Ibid., p. 117.

[7] Ibid. Cf. Ellul's "Nature, Technique, and Artificiality," pp. 273-275.

Yet, freedom always has been and continues to be the universal aspiration, "the supreme goal," of all people.[8] In fact, according to Ellul, freedom is one of the primary values which the west has bequeathed to the entire world.[9] Unfortunately, we have squandered and betrayed this precious legacy to the point that the loss of freedom and the unilateral triumph of necessity have reached epidemic and unprecedented proportions. Our current dilemma is totally new and different, far more dangerous than it has ever been.[10]

Several Ellul interpreters have recognized the centrality and primacy of freedom for Ellul's thought. Brian McGreevy writes that, for Ellul, freedom is "the _sine_ _qua_ _non_ of meaningful human existence."[11] Daniel Cérézuelle, a former student of Ellul's, shows how Ellul's basic project revolves around "the extent to which technique undermines human freedom."[12] We could document many more examples. John Schaar, Norman Brown, John Badertscher and others all recognize that, for Ellul, the

---

[8]Idem, "Conformism and the Rationale of Technique," p. 98. Ellul makes this same point in his article "La Peur de la liberté," _Sud-Ouest Dimanche_ (November 18, 1979): 5, but goes on to argue that, even so, most people refuse to accept the heavy responsibilities which freedom imposes on them.

[9]Idem, _Betrayal_, pp. 17-20, 82, 132, and 144.

[10]Ellul makes this point in several places. See FPOK, p. 8, and _The Political Illusion_, pp. 226ff.

[11]Brian McGreevy, "Ellul and the Supreme Court on Freedom," _Christian Legal Society Quarterly_ 4, nos. 2-3 (1983): 31.

[12]Daniel Cérézuelle, "From the Technical Phenomenon to the Technical System," in _Research in Philosophy and Technology_, Vol. 3, p. 162. As Cérézuelle points out in the introduction to this article, for Ellul, the technological society "tends to form a total, if not totalitarian, order--a society progressively integrated as a function of a technical logic which can only drain away human liberty in the search for power, efficiency, and organization..." (p. 162).

dilemma of modern society revolves around the loss of freedom to the growing determinisms of the technological society.[13]

Freedom, then, is crucial to Ellul's thought. It is the one value which he regards as more important than any other.[14] As one perceptive interviewer put it when addressing Ellul, "Everything which touches upon human freedom is particularly dear to you."[15] Ellul readily admits this and confesses that "nothing I have done, experienced, or thought makes sense if it is not considered in the light of freedom."[16] In fact, the urgency of the current situation influenced Ellul to begin his three-part ethic, which is based upon the Pauline virtues of faith, hope, and love, with freedom (the ethical aspect of hope). In the words of David Gill, for Ellul, freedom and hope "are the greatest needs in our hopeless era."[17] They take on a special urgency and importance. To its own peril, the church has neglected, ignored and rejected this crucial orientation, to

---

[13]See John Schaar, "Jacques Ellul: Between Babylon and the New Jerusalem," Democracy, vol. 2, no. 4 (Fall 1982): 103-105, 108, and 110; Norman O. Brown, "Jacques Ellul: Beyond Geneva and Jerusalem," Democracy, vol. 2, no. 4 (Fall 1982): 123-124; and John Badertscher, "George P. Grant and Jacques Ellul on Freedom in a Technological Society," in George Grant in Process: Essays and Conversations, Larry Schmidt, ed. (Toronto: House of Anansi, 1978), pp. 86-88. Others who acknowledge the crucial status of freedom in Ellul's thought include Outka (p. 189), Fasching in his book (p. 53), and the dissertations by Burke (p. 14) and especially Wren (pp. 5, 229-230, 290, and 299).

[14]Ellul, "Conformism and the Rationale of Technique," p. 101.

[15]Marie-Claire Lescaze, "Une Interview de Jacques Ellul: Les Marges de la liberté en Occident," La Vie Protestante 43 (February 29, 1980): 1.

[16]Ellul, ISOS, p. 183.

[17]Gill, in the "Introduction" to Ellul's Living Faith, p. xii. See The Ethics of Freedom (p. 7), where Ellul explains his projected three-part ethic, centered around the Pauline virtues. There he also writes that holiness and love are possible "only on the basis and in terms of the functioning of freedom." For the relationship between freedom and hope, see The Ethics of Freedom (pp. 12-19) and Hope (pp. 239-242).

the point that freedom has become a trivialized commonplace.[18] Ellul attempts to restore it to what he feels is its only proper role. This chapter analyzes just what he means by his "freedom."

2. Ellul on liberation theology

Although we will make occasional references to other thinkers on the subject of freedom, we must restrict ourselves to Ellul's own thought. Our goal is to determine what Ellul, not all of western intellectual history, has said on the subject. Anyone interested in the latter can begin with Mortimer Adler's massive work, The Idea of Freedom, a book we will incorporate on several occasions.[19] We can begin, however, by at least locating Ellul within the discussion about freedom which has taken place within theology.

Although the church has historically had a reputation, often deserved, for being intolerant, oppressive, imperialistic, and authoritarian,[20] freedom has been one of its major themes, especially in recent years with the advent of liberation theology. The list of authors who have written on the subject, both from a more "traditional" vantage point (Luther, Küng, Thielicke, Robert Osborne, Käsemann, and so on), and from the position of liberation vis-à-vis race (William Jones, James

---

[18] On the one hand, in 1975, Ellul wrote that freedom was a theme which found "so little place in the teaching of the church" and that "it is a theme which has vanished from the Christian horizon" (The Ethics of Freedom, p. 105; cf. p. 108, n. 3). On the other hand, in 1985, he wrote that to talk about freedom has become commonplace and trivial ("L'Antidestin," p. 113). His several books, FPOK, A Critique of the New Commonplaces, and Autopsy of Revolution, support this second view. Ellul either contradicts himself, or, more likely, means by "neglect" the idea that freedom has been "misconstrued."

[19] Mortimer J. Adler, The Idea of Freedom: A Dialectical Examination of the Conceptions of Freedom (Westport, CT.: Greenwood Press, 1958). Adler writes that this work attempts to be a comprehensive and non-partisan examination of "25 centuries of recorded thought on that subject" (p. xix). His book proffers three broad categories of freedom (circumstantial, acquired, and natural), to each of which corresponds a "mode of the self" (self-realization, self-perfection, and self-determination).

[20] Ellul, "La Croix et la liberté," Le Christianisme au XX Siècle, no. 11 (March 15, 1982): 5. Compare our remarks in footnote #18 above.

93

Cone), gender (Letty Russell, Mary Daly, Elizabeth Fiorenza, and Rosemary Reuther), and the socio-economic factors (Boff, Bonino, Gutierrez), is almost endless. We cannot possibly hope to do justice to this vast body of literature in this short chapter. Suffice it to say that Ellul has a vested interest in many of the same concerns of liberation theology, little interest in traditional or dogmatic conceptions of the problem, and an approach which attempts to steer something of a middle course between the two. He even makes the bold claim that in 1946, with his The Presence of the Kingdom, he was one of the very first to formulate a "theology of revolution."[21] His quarrel with liberation theology expresses itself in at least four points.

First, although it is good that theology is "shaped by the problems of the times,"[22] and even unthinkable that it would be otherwise,[23] Ellul complains that too much of liberation theology is totally unoriginal in its perspective. It reveals "customary...startling conformity" to sociological trends.[24] That is, theologians are often tag-alongs or Johnny-come-latelies who are eager to jump on the latest bandwagon. They proffer nothing at all new or creative, and instead merely parrot stock cliches and phrases. Second, and closely related to this first point, Ellul charges that much theology of revolution is overly theoretical and totally unrealistic. For example, although he himself has chosen to identify with the poor and disenfranchised of the world, he rejects any mere sentimentality toward the poor which makes of them a value an sich, or any notion that a particular political party is "the party of the poor." He castigates what he feels constitutes gross mediocrity and incompetence in many church pronouncements. As we noted before, the worst and most unfortunate example of these first two points is the World Council of Churches, whose declarations he has

---

[21] Idem, Autopsy, p. 218, n. 23. Pages 217-232 of this book examine "The Theology of Revolution." See Chapter II of POK, entitled "Revolutionary Christianity."

[22] Idem, Violence, p. 28.

[23] Idem, FPOK, p. 90. Ellul's own personal life verifies these last two statements. Vanderburg is certainly accurate when he writes in the introduction to POOA, "Ellul is not an ivory-tower intellectual who formulates his critique from a safe distance. His thought is an integral part of his life..."

[24] Idem, Autopsy, pp. 219-220. See pp. 217, 225.

characterized as "a tissue of platitudes, prefabricated notions, and sociological or historical errors."[25]

Third, Ellul rejects any form of violence or violent means to achieve any liberation. Means always effect ends and sometimes usurp them. Violence only begets further violence, even as it rejects and forfeits reconciliation. So-called "Christian" violence is never justified, according to Ellul. It simply constitutes another will to power. Of course, not all liberation theology advocates violence, but that which does incurs Ellul's wrath. Fourth, Ellul criticizes much liberation theology for what we might call its lack of Christian specificity.[26] When revolution usurps faith, when theological virtues cease to have meaningful content except within a political context, or when faith and freedom are relegated to and depend upon purely external circumstances, then Christians have become what he calls "realists" in the worst sense of the term. That is, they reveal a this-world-only mentality which evidences a total lack of a uniquely Christian perspective.[27]

Thus, Ellul writes that "the so-called theologies of liberation and of revelation are, of course, the very opposite of what I mean here by the practice of liberty, since they are based on political illusion and on the opium of the intellectuals."[28] In an excellent two-part article, Thomas Hanks shows how, on the one hand, Ellul is the "original liberation theologian," a true precursor to the more modern movement who was "born both before his time and geographically out of place," and how, on the other hand, Ellul transcends much of liberation theology.[29] Thus, while Ellul aligns himself with many of the same concerns of liberation theology, he approaches them in his own, unique way.

---

[25] Ibid., p. 226.

[26] Idem, Violence, p. 70.

[27] Idem, Prayer and Modern Man, p. 75. Jesus, for example, resisted the temptation to elevate material factors to a sacrosanct level in his temptation. See The Ethics of Freedom (pp. 52-57).

[28] Idem, "Technology and the Gospel," International Review of Missions 66, no. 262 (April 1977): 117, n. 4.

[29] See his two articles, "Jacques Ellul: The Original 'Liberation Theologian,'" and "How Ellul Transcends Liberation Theologies," both of which appear in TSF Bulletin (1984) and which have been cited previously.

In keeping with Hanks' request for an explication of Ellul's "analysis of authentic liberation,"[30] we can now outline the course of this chapter. After examining some misconceptions and illusions surrounding the idea of freedom, we will posit the sources of freedom, the objects from which we are liberated, and then the orientation or parameters of freedom. A conclusion completes the chapter.

B. Towards a Definition of Freedom: Illusions and Misconceptions

Ellul writes that it is both difficult and easy to define freedom.[31] In one sense, it is easy. In the reference just cited, for example, Ellul refers to Augustine's famous dictum as a possible starting point: Love God and do what you please. Likewise, in several places he proffers short, simple definitions of liberty. Freedom, he writes, is "uniquely an ethical expression of the liberation effected by God for man in Jesus Christ."[32] Or, "freedom, the freedom, which God gives, is to be understood from the very first as a power or possibility. It is a power to act and to obey. It is a possibility of life and strength for combat."[33]

In another sense, however, it is difficult to define freedom. Ellul felt compelled to write over 500 pages on the matter. Further, he continually argues that it is not only impossible but undesirable to construct any one system or expression of the Christian faith. Each individual person must craft his own style of life, depending upon his or her own circumstances, time, and personal conscience. Thus, freedom will necessarily assume various and differing forms. For this reason it is difficult to define. In this section we can work toward a definition by disabusing ourselves of what Ellul would call illusions and misconceptions.

---

[30] Hanks, "How Ellul Transcends Liberation Theologies," p. 15. Except for McGreevy's short article, half of which is devoted to the view of the U.S. Supreme Court, and the article by Badertscher, half of which considers George Grant's view of freedom, I have not found any articles which attempt to fulfill Hanks' request.

[31] Ellul, "Le Sens," p. 7.

[32] Idem, Hope, p. 240. The emphasis is Ellul's.

[33] Idem, The Ethics of Freedom, p. 103.

1. Illusions of freedom

Ellul's major writings have focused on several illusions of freedom. Technique proffers humanity what Badertscher calls a "false freedom," for the "technological society uses freedom as a slogan to hide the reality of ever-increasing necessity."[34] Take computer technology, for example. Theoretically, computers could be an instrument of freedom. They save time, are more efficient, and so on. Ellul, however, makes several points. Computers create an aristocratic elite out of the technicians who use and program them. This tends to diminish the importance of the non-computer expert. Computers tend to label people, and, once pigeon-holed, the individual can be marked for life. For a Christian, Ellul also warns that computers minimize interpersonal relationships. In the end, the suggestion that computers increase our freedom is just another superficial thought.[35]

Ellul's two works Propaganda and The Humiliation of the Word are wholly devoted to a second illusion of freedom created by what he calls "the triumph of the image."[36] The triumph of the image, best exemplified in propaganda, creates the awareness of non-reality and the non-awareness of reality. The problem here rests in one's total absorption with false reality whereby one "gives oneself over to the illusory, to illusion actually, which one takes to be the real."[37] As a result, people rest confidently in a host of false freedoms.

Politics, to take a third example, offers the supreme illusion of freedom. Political liberalism, for example, is what Bernard Charbonneau, one of Ellul's favorite authors, has called

---

[34] Badertscher, pp. 86-87. Cf. Boli-Bennett, p. 182.

[35] Ellul, "L'Homme et l'ordinateur," Evangile et Liberté 94.1 (January 7, 1980): 8-9. Ellul makes similar remarks in his interview, "Les Marges de la liberté en Occident," p 1. For other remarks by Ellul on computers, see The Technological System, pp. 73-74, and 93-015.

[36] Idem, Hope, p. 35.

[37] Ibid., p. 36.

"the lie of liberty."[38] Ellul's two books <u>False Presence of the Kingdom</u> and <u>The Political Illusion</u> are given to this third illusion.[39] Fourth, we can mention the illusion of freedom through revolution, the subject of Ellul's work <u>Autopsy of Revolution</u>. Far from being an agent of liberation, revolution has been trivialized, domesticated, and, to use Richard Schickel's apt term, "co-opted" by "the very structure against which, traditionally, it was directed--namely, the state."[40] According to Ellul, "we know how many times revolutions made in the name of freedom have eventually led to dictators and prisons," to the exact opposite of their ostensible goal.[41] As is all too common in these four illusions, what people call freedom is often its very opposite, oppression and necessity.[42]

---

[38]The title of Charbonneau's book is <u>Le Mensonge de la liberté</u>. Cf. Ellul's comments in <u>The Ethics of Freedom</u>, p. 274, and in "L'Antidestin," p. 116. In a footnote to his article "Nature, Technique, and Artificiality," Ellul calls this book by Charbonneau "the most profound analysis of our age and society-- but one which has never been able to find a publisher" (p. 283, n. 9).

[39]As Fasching observes, for Ellul, "politics is the point of convergence for technique and propaganda in this society. This is the point where they coalesce to create the illusion of freedom--the illusion of the control of technology through politics, by means of which technology seems to be an instrument of human freedom." See his <u>The Thought of Jacques Ellul</u>, pp. 26-27.

[40]Richard Schickel, "Marx is Dead," <u>Harper's</u> 244 (April 1972): 96.

[41]Ellul, "La Peur de la liberté," p. 5.

[42]Idem, <u>The Ethics of Freedom</u>, p. 273. As one other example of this phenomenon, we can take Ellul's example that "liberating" revolutions most always leave the state "enlarged, better organized, more potent, and with wider areas of influence...It is a matter of record which no theory can disprove" (<u>Autopsy</u>, p. 160). For other examples of illusions of freedom, see the four pertinent chapters of <u>A Critique of the New Commonplaces</u> (pp. 149-178); <u>The Ethics of Freedom</u> (pp. 230-231), where Ellul mentions the illusions of freedom which society offers through fantasy, leisure, vacations, sports, television, and politics; and Ellul's review of the film <u>Le Fantôme de la liberté</u>, entitled "La Liberté dénaturée," <u>Réforme</u> 1551 (December 7, 1974): 14-15, which film he calls "a marvelous illustration of the perversion of freedom."

2. Misconceptions about freedom

In addition to these illusions of freedom, Ellul is convinced that we harbor many misconceptions about its true nature. While these illusions of freedom provide concrete examples from real life, the following misconceptions are more conceptual. Dispersed throughout his books and articles, we can cull out at least seven misconceptions about freedom. By doing this we can narrow our focus on Ellul's own definition which follows in the succeeding sections of this chapter.

(1) Adler mentions one commonly held view of freedom which posits that it is natural or inherent in all people from birth, regardless of their station in life, external circumstances, particular state of mind or character, and so on.[43] We recall, for example, the famous opening lines of Rousseau's Social Contract, that all people are born with a natural freedom in the state of nature. Ellul categorically rejects such a view, contending instead that freedom is not continuous with human nature, but that it is discontinuous with it and "based on a rupture with human nature."[44] That is, human freedom for Ellul is what we could call "derivative" and not innate, something "acquired," to use Adler's category. Because of our inborn enslavement to sin, and to the all-embracing, closed system which technique has created, freedom must and can only come from a Wholly Other which transcends this system. Thus, Ellul argues that true freedom comes "from the outside" (de l'extérieur) or "from somewhere apart from us" (d'ailleurs).[45] In another place he compares it to a piece of clothing which is put on a person. In other words, "what is required if freedom is to be possible is the intervention of the Wholly Other, of that which has nothing in common with human nature, of that which is not subject to necessity."[46] Thus, freedom is not

---

[43] Adler, p. 149. Adler's "representative list" of people who have espoused this view includes 32 different people (p. 148).

[44] Ellul, "Le Sens," p. 10. He makes this point in several different places. See "Technology and the Gospel," p. 117; The Ethics of Freedom, p. 11; Prayer, p. 121; and The Technological Society, p. xxxii.

[45] Idem, "La Croix et la liberté," p. 5.

[46] Idem, The Ethics of Freedom, p. 72. Cf. pp. 342-343. McGreevy recognizes this point, that freedom, for Ellul, is possible only through a relationship with the transcendent (p. 28), who alone is the guarantee of freedom. Cf. POOA, p. 102, and The Politics of God and the Politics of Man, p. 142.

something which is ours at birth or by nature. It depends solely on a derivative source, God, and is based on his own pure freedom. It is like the emancipation granted to a Roman slave, which depends solely on the grace of his master.[47]

(2) We mentioned before at several places that for Ellul the question of freedom is not a metaphysical problem. On this level, the question is simply a useless and insoluble debate. According to him, "Holy Scripture absolutely does not help us to resolve the problem of metaphysical freedom."[48] To pose the problem on this metaphysical level is totally counterproductive, a false problem which we can never hope to solve. For Ellul, the important and correct framework for the problem of freedom is the ethical or existential. As in all his work, Ellul continually steers away from the theoretical, the speculative, or the purely dogmatic formulation of an issue, and turns his attention to the practical, concrete arena of life. In Gill's words, this is simply Ellul's "lifelong attempt to move beyond abstract orthodoxy to concrete engagement with the world."[49] Freedom, then, in Ellul's thought, is an ethical and not a metaphysical problem.

(3) Ellul also contends that freedom is not the mere ability to make choices. He criticizes this view as "the most formal and simplistic concept of freedom...In reality this concept of freedom is very superficial."[50] In other words, people might be independent, and have the option of several choices, but this hardly means that they are free. In the technological society, Ellul argues, choices are artificial, predetermined and limited. The dice are loaded before we "choose." We make decisions and choices, of course, but these are only what Ellul calls "pseudo-decisions" which are rigorously determined beforehand. Who has not complained, for example, of having no true choice in a political election, despite the presence of a dozen, very different candidates? Christian freedom, the type which Ellul will espouse, is doggedly realistic about sociological conformity. It is truly

---

[47] Idem, "Le Sens," pp. 16, 19.

[48] Ibid., p. 4. Cf. "L'Antidestin," p. 113, and "La Croix et la liberté," p. 6.

[49] Gill, in Ellul's Living Faith, p. xv. See footnote #26 of chapter 3 above for further references to this theme.

[50] Ellul, The Ethics of Freedom, p. 113. Pages 112-119 of this book are entitled "Freedom and Choice."

creative, moving beyond the trite notion that freedom consists of simple choice.[51]

(4) In the last chapter we made a distinction which we can but recall here. For Ellul, freedom is never collective, but only individual. Adler designates a group who contend that freedom is collective, represented in such people as Comte, Bakunin, Marx and Engels.[52] With his keen focus on Kierkegaard's stress on radical subjectivity and the strategic importance of "the single individual," Ellul rejects any such notion. "Freedom is indeed an individual act and lifestyle. There is no collective freedom and Christ has not liberated man or mankind in general."[53] Freedom must be fought for and taken up by each individual person. Authentic revolution, for example, could only begin by rejecting "the mounting ascendancy of groups over individuals" and by moving towards "the rediscovery of individual autonomy [and] the redemption of individuality."[54] Any view of freedom which forgets this fundamental distinction is, in Ellul's view, wrongheaded.

(5) We should not imagine that freedom, even the freedom which God gives to the individual, is pure, absolute or permanent. Freedom is not an inalienable gift which issues forth in a theologia gloria and which can never be lost. Ellul makes several important distinctions on this point. First, if the single individual does not assume and fight for his freedom, if he does not exercise this gift of God and "work out his salvation with fear and trembling," then he cannot expect a magical bestowal of liberty from on high. Salvation, for Ellul,

---

[51]See The Technological System, pp. 319-325, where Ellul discusses the matter of freedom and choice. McGreevy also notes this point in his article (p. 27).

[52]Adler, pp. 370-399.

[53]Ellul, The Ethics of Freedom, p. 270. Ellul goes on to say, though, that if a Christian does not assume and act out his freedom, the unfortunate consequences do effect the collective whole of society.

[54]Idem, Autopsy, pp. 275, 281-282. Cf. Ellul's "Between Chaos and Paralysis," pp. 748-749. We might recall Kierkegaard's continual contrast between the homogeneous crowd and the solitary person.

80476

does not necessarily entail freedom, although the latter is never possible without the former.[55]

In addition, we must always keep in mind Ellul's constant distinction between the Already and the Not Yet of God's kingdom. The work of Christ, which forms the source of freedom, is universal, radical, total, and actual, but it is also hidden, not fully expressed, suspended, and secret.[56] The freedom of a Christian, then, will never be fully perfected or lived out until the final eschaton.

Thus, freedom is not a magical gift which is automatically bestowed upon a Christian in salvation. As "the most precious thing of our lives,"[57] it must be guarded, nourished, protected and exercised. It is not an automatic privilege, but something which imposes upon the believer an incredible responsibility, a responsibility so severe that many refuse to accept it. While all people aspire to freedom, few are willing to take the risks, the fatigue, and efforts it requires. People naturally prefer the comfort and security of the status quo. They actually have what Ellul calls "the fear of freedom." Freedom, therefore, "is never established once and for all; it has to be constantly reconquered, lost, and gambled for again....[It demands] the necessity of constantly renewed action."[58] In conclusion, freedom is a fragile thing, something which is "never stable, never is it acquired, and it is necessary to know that even an instant of freedom comes at great cost."[59]

(6) Our last two distinctions are reciprocally related. Ellul argues that freedom is not something which is merely an inward or purely "spiritual" experience which is unrelated to external, concrete constraints. The entire doctrine of the incarnation militates against such a view. True freedom

---

[55] Idem, The Ethics of Freedom, p. 83. Cf. p. 15. In "L'Sens," for example, we learn that a Christian can lose his freedom when it is separated from love of neighbor and the glory of God (p. 20).

[56] Ibid., pp. 83-85.

[57] Idem, "L'Sens," p. 20.

[58] Idem, ISOS, p. 222. Note the explicit Kierkegaardian emphasis on risk and faith as a gamble. On this entire section, recall the struggle of St. Paul in Romans 7.

[59] Idem, "La Peur de la liberté," p. 5.

embraces all of life, the spiritual and the material. It is holistic and intersects the concrete political and social realities of our lives.[60] Two examples illustrate this point.

Christians do not exercise political freedom by withdrawing from that arena, as tempting as that might be. To do so would only have the opposite effect of the one intended, for it would only grant the state more unrestrained power and influence, the end result being the further restriction of personal freedom. According to Ellul, true freedom obliges one to take his or her place fully in the concrete socio-political realities of everyday life. Prayer, to take another example, one of the supreme acts of freedom according to Ellul, does not absolve one from engagement with the world. Precisely the opposite is true. There can be no true prayer without vigorous action.[61]

To relegate freedom to the purely spiritual or inward domain is a tragic misconception of its true nature. Ellul devotes the entire Part IV of his Ethics of Freedom to showing the concrete implications of Christian freedom in the spheres of politics, the state, revolution, religion, family, work, sex, money, and vocation. Any dichotomy of the concrete and the spiritual represents both an evasion of responsibility and a superficial view of freedom.

(7) On the other hand, however, Ellul takes care to say that freedom does not depend entirely or necessarily on external circumstances. That is, freedom does not mean a total absence of restraint, limits, or necessity. It is not simply autonomy or the ability to do whatever one desires. The perfect freedom of Christ in the midst of his three temptations, temptations which sum up and far surpass any of those which we might encounter, perfectly illustrates this.[62] In several places Ellul criticizes liberation theology for failing to see this point, and for supposing that freedom is absolutely impossible unless adverse external circumstances are removed. This in no way means, as we have seen, that he devalues the importance of

---

[60]See "La Croix et la liberté" (p. 6) and "Le Sens" (pp. 9-10).

[61]Ellul, Prayer, pp. 160-164, and 170-175.

[62]Idem, The Ethics of Freedom, pp. 13, 74-75. See Adler's chapter 4, where he considers "Circumstantial Freedom," the idea that "an individual's possession of freedom somehow depends on the external circumstances under which he lives and tries to act" (The Idea of Freedom, p. 110).

those external constraints. He only wants us to see them in their proper perspective.

Freedom exists not in the absence of necessity but always and only in dialectical tension with it. "We know freedom only when we have to struggle against a destiny."[63] In one place he uses the illustration of gravity and the corresponding problems incurred with weightlessness. Or, freedom is like the yachtsman who negotiates the contrary wind and waves, and whose only dread is the absolute calm.[64] It is like the poet who grapples with the rules of language which, if they did not exist, would create an intolerable situation.[65] In the Foreward to The Technological Society, Ellul writes that "reality is itself a combination of determinisms, and freedom consists in overcoming and transcending these determinisms. Freedom is completely without meaning unless it is related to necessity, unless it represents victory over necessity."[66]

Having attempted to disabuse ourselves of some common misconceptions about and illusions of freedom, we are now in a position to examine its source. We have already hinted that for Ellul all human freedom comes from God alone. To be more specific, all human freedom has as its source the incarnate and inscripturated word of God. In what follows, our purpose is not to produce a thorough analysis of Ellul's christology or doctrine of scripture. Others have done this well enough.[67]

---

[63] Idem, "Nature, Technique and Artificiality," pp. 277-278. Cf. Betrayal, pp. 26-27.

[64] Idem, The Ethics of Freedom, p. 233.

[65] Idem, The Political Illusion, p. 212.

[66] Idem, The Technological Society, p. xxxii. Cf. "La Liberté dénaturée," p. 14. We can see more clearly, therefore, what Ellul means when in his article "Between Chaos and Paralysis" he says that our problem is the absence of tensions, and that the duty of Christians is to reintroduce fruitful tensions into society by proffering truly unique and creative styles of life.

[67] On Ellul's christology, see Gill's The Word of God in the Ethics of Jacques Ellul (pp. 59-67), and Temple's dissertation (pp. 354-376). On his doctrine of scripture, see Gill's article, "Jacques Ellul's View of Scripture," Journal of the Evangelical Theological Society 25 (December 1982): 467-478, and the long section of Temple's dissertation (pp. 207-309).

We simply want to show how these two doctrines are strategically related to our subject of freedom as its ultimate source.

C. Freedom-By: The Source of Freedom

1. The freedom of God and of Jesus Christ

The source of human freedom, having described it as something which is acquired or derivative and not as something natural or inherent in all people at birth, is God, who alone is perfectly free. God's freedom, unlike our own, is absolute and unrestricted, "counselled and controlled by nobody."[68] Ellul tells us that this idea is one which he directly credits to Barth, whose genius was to show the dialectical relation between the freedom of God and humanity. Disclaiming any speculative, metaphysical interest in this relationship, Ellul insists that it is a most practical subject, and his book The Politics of God and the Politics of Man is wholly devoted to it.

According to Ellul, God always and only reveals himself as the liberator. Above all else (avant tout), God shows himself as the God who frees his people. Before revealing himself as Creator, Judge, or the omnipotent one, God reveals himself as "the one who frees, not only from slavery, but from everything."[69] As the truly free One, he desires above all that his creatures and his creation be "free before him in order to love and adore him."[70] We can say, then, that in general all our freedom has as its source the perfect freedom of God. In particular, this expresses itself in the person and work of Christ and in Holy Scripture.

In Jesus Christ, the Wholly Other God becomes man, taking his place beside us and among us. He removes and bridges the infinite chasm or abyss which separated us. We can know God fully only in this Jesus, who, according to Ellul, is the perfect source and paradigm of freedom: "Free, he chose to keep the law. Free, he chose to live out the will of God. Free, he

---

[68] Idem, The Politics of God and the Politics of Man, p. 59.

[69] Idem, "La Croix et la liberté," p. 5. Ellul makes this same point in several places. See "L'Antidestin," (p. 119), and "Technology and the Gospel" (p. 116).

[70] Ibid., p. 6.

chose the incarnation. Free, he chose to die."[71] The story
of his threefold temptation illustrates this marvelously.

Ellul does not flinch at all in affirming the obvious
implication: apart from participation in the work of Christ, a
person cannot be truly free. Thus, as Bromiley notes, "freedom
is received exclusively in Christ," and nowhere else.[72] Jesus
"accomplishes in a decisive, unique, and irreversible manner,
and for eternity, the Father's plan of liberation."[73] Ellul
suggests that this work of Christ is best understood today as a
work of liberation. While the idea of redemption was adequate
and accurate for the first few centuries, drawing as it does
upon the idea of the manumission of a slave, today the figure
tends to obscure and confuse the issue. A more adequate modern
equivalent pictures Christ's work as the triumph of liberation.
Ellul's intention here is not to reinterpret the work of Christ,
but to focus our attention on what he feels is its primary
impact.

At any rate, "In Jesus Christ [God] accomplishes for man
liberty in its totality."[74] He vanquishes destiny and makes
true freedom possible in every sphere of life. The emancipation
he proffers touches all the forms of slavery and necessity that
sin had taken: "Jesus frees everywhere He passes; He frees from
sickness, from demons, from false beliefs, from servitude to the
powers of the world, money, political power, and morality."[75]
In short, the beginning point of any and all freedom rests in a
personal participation in the liberating work of Christ.

2. The freedom of the Word of God

Although for Ellul freedom means, first of all, confessing
Christ as Lord and Saviour, it also implies knowing the Scriptures. The two are inseparable.[76] All of Scripture in its
entirety is a great book about liberation. "The whole thought

---

[71] Idem, The Ethics of Freedom, p. 51.

[72] Bromiley, p. 42. See "Le Sens," p. 5.

[73] Ellul, "L'Antidestin," p. 120.

[74] Idem, "Technology and the Gospel," p. 116.

[75] Idem, "L'Antidestin," p. 122.

[76] Idem, The Ethics of Freedom, p. 87.

of Scripture," the entire Jewish Bible, all the traditional thought of the Hebrews, and all revelation in Israel centers around this controlling theme that God is the God who frees.[77] According to Ellul, "Freedom is the basic theme which ties everything else in the Bible together, from beginning to end."[78] Many theologians have missed this point, Ellul thinks. They make freedom one part of the Biblical message. He cites Bonhoeffer as an example. For Ellul, freedom is not one part of the Biblical message, but its very essence. Käsemann is one of the rare exceptions, he feels, and is one who has truly captured the import of this.[79]

The Exodus under the leadership of Moses constituted "the first explosion" of God's liberating power, the guarantee and promise of all other liberation.[80] The prophets and the historical books continue with "a single thing," that God frees his people, whether it be from political bondage in Egypt or Babylon, from idols, from the slavery of the law, or from the tyranny of the state (1 Samuel 8).[81] Each biblical writer approaches this common theme from a slightly different angle. In the Johannine corpus, we learn of freedom from the world, from sin and its slavery. Paul writes about freedom from the flesh and from the law. Isaiah and Deuteronomy inform us of a freedom "in relation to the work of our hands." Exodus focuses on freedom from the powers.[82]

---

[77] Idem, The Ethics of Freedom, p. 98; "La Croix et la liberté," p. 5; "L'Antidestin," p. 120; and "Le Sens," pp. 3-4.

[78] Idem, Humiliation, p. 58.

[79] See Ernst Käsemann, Jesus Means Freedom, trans. by Frank Clark (Philadelphia: Fortress Press, 1977). Käsemann proposes that "the whole of the New Testament" focuses on freedom (pp. 9-10). His book is an attempt to show how this is so. According to him, the "essential nature of the church" is simply "the freedom of God's children" (pp. 11, 15). Like Ellul, Käsemann argues that freedom is not something natural or ready-made at birth, but something for which we must struggle and which is only given in Christ (p. 48).

[80] Ellul, "L'Antidestin," p. 118; "Le Sens," p. 4.

[81] Idem, "Le Sens," pp. 3-4.

[82] Idem, The Ethics of Freedom, p. 133.

While all of scripture in its totality has as its theme the
liberation which God gives, Paul in particular is the theologian
of freedom par excellence. He was the first to picture the work
of Christ as one of emancipation, and the Christian life as one
of former slaves made free. According to Ellul's arithmetic,
the terms relating to freedom occur about 40 times in Paul's
writings and about 18 times in the rest of the New Testament.[83]
More than any other Biblical author, Paul expounds upon the
nature of Christian freedom. For Paul, freedom is not one of
the Christian virtues among others, but the essential nature of
the Christian life, the climate and setting of all the other
virtues: "Without this liberty there is no Christian
life." [84] In his comprehensive exposition of the subject,
Paul tells us of a freedom not only from the law, but also from
the powers, the state, work, money, and, in short, from all the
various forms of slavery which necessity takes.

In conclusion, the source of freedom rests uniquely in the
liberating work of Jesus Christ, and in the witness of Holy
Scripture to it. Whenever people receive and accept the witness
of Holy Scripture, "man has a freedom and power which fulfill
human pretensions and which correspond to the power and freedom
of the Word of God itself."[85] Ellul readily embraces the
obvious corollary that Christians alone can be free. According
to him, freedom will never come through violence which seeks to
destroy oppressive powers, love, the "rule of the right,"
economic justice or technique. These only represent illusions
and misconceptions. They actually have destroyed freedom, a

---

[83]These are the figures which Ellul uses in his article,
"Le Sens," first written in 1951. In The Ethics of Freedom,
written in 1975, he figures that the themes of liberation "occur
about sixty times in Paul as compared with only twenty-five
times in the rest of the New Testament" (p. 95).

[84]Ellul, "Le Sens," p. 7.

[85]Idem, The Ethics of Freedom, p. 66. Compare his
similar remarks in The New Demons, where he writes that "the
Christian revelation has once again to play its role as negator
and destroyer of the sacred obsessions, of the religious phan-
tasmagoria, in order to liberate man" (pp. 227-228); and "If,
then, we too can live as free men in Christ, this is because of
the word of God. The only true, complete, absolute, and
intrinsic freedom is that of the word of God. For this word is
the basis and ground of our freedom, as it was of the freedom of
Jesus himself" (The Ethics of Freedom, p. 62).

charge which he feels is a simple fact of history.[86] The freedom of God, given in Jesus Christ as found in the witness of Holy Scripture, is the only source of final liberation. Because of Him, destiny and necessity have been vanquished. Ellul even goes so far as to say that all genuine movements of freedom, even non-Christian ones, have their roots in the Judeo-Christian heritage of the liberator God. They are simply by-products made possible by the latter.[87] Badertscher summarizes the whole matter of the source of freedom in this way:

> Freedom enters the human situation with the revelation of God to whom the Bible bears witness. God, in his radical freedom, confronts man with his gracious word, which is both a command and an invitation to fellowship. The intervention of God in human history through the life, death and resurrection of Jesus Christ breaks the power of necessity and gives all human beings the choice of fellowship with him.[88]

With this in mind, we can now move on to the objects of freedom, that is, to an examination of that from which God frees his people.

D. Freedom-From

1. The objective/external

Although Ellul addresses this issue differently in various writings, we can say, using the delineation alluded to above, that Jesus Christ frees us from both the objective/external and subjective/internal factors which enslave us. That is, freedom is neither merely spiritual nor exclusively material. For

---

[86]Idem, "Le Peur de la liberté," p. 5.

[87]Idem, "L'Antidestin," p. 122. This is so because, as David Gill says, in Ellul's christology, "the incarnation, death and resurrection of Jesus Christ are the focal point and the critical influence on everything that was, is, and will be on earth and in heaven--all of history is modified, social relations are changed, transcendent reality is decided, all by this event." See his The Word of God in the Ethics of Jacques Ellul, p. 67. The emphasis is his own.

[88]Badertscher, pp. 87-88. For Ellul's contention that only Christians can be free, see The Ethics of Freedom, pp. 84, 86, and 272-273, and "Le Sens," p. 7.

Ellul, both are true and inseparable. On the one hand, Jesus Christ liberates us from the external bondage of the "powers" and from the "effects" of necessity. On the other hand, he also frees us from the inward slavery to ourselves, represented in the biblical idea of the "flesh."

Because of Jesus Christ, the outward effects of necessity, all the determinisms created in the original cleavage of sin, no longer need constrain a person, at least not in the sense in which they did prior to one's Christian conversion. Jesus Christ conquers destiny and fate. There is no longer any fatality or uncontestable determinism, for Christ has once and for all broken the impenetrable, closed system. Ellul suggests that this is true on an <u>objective</u> level, a level which requires our subjective participation for its full effect, but which is nevertheless true even without it.[89] For the first time, real possibility, truly meaningful choices, and creativity in decisions are possible, all because of the work of Christ. The domains of work, the state, money, and so on, once the exclusive realm of strict necessity, are now possible domains of liberty.[90]

Secondly, on the objective/external level, the work of God in Christ frees the individual from the "powers" (<u>exousiai</u>). Ellul recognizes four main interpretations of these "powers:" (1) demons, in the literal, simplistic sense of the word; (2) less precise beings, but forces which nevertheless have an objective reality; (3) "a disposition of man which constitutes this or that human factor a power by exalting it as such;"[91] and (4) a figure of speech.

Ellul makes several points in forming his own opinion. First, he dismisses as "altogether superficial" the professional critics of the Bible who construe the "powers" as the magical talk of a primitive culture which requires our scientific, come-of-age demythologizing.[92] This attitude reflects his whole stance toward scripture which, while it accepts higher criticism as a useful tool when it is kept in its place, rejects

---

[89] Ellul, "L'Antidestin," p. 121. Compare footnote #87 above and the statement by Gill about Ellul's christology.

[90] Idem, "Le Sens," p. 6.

[91] Idem, The Ethics of Freedom, p. 151.

[92] Idem, Violence, p. 162.

the hubris and pretensions of many modern scholars.[93] For Ellul, not the Bible, but the modern world, needs demythologizing. We have no right, as Barth says, to look over the shoulders of the biblical authors as a teacher, benevolently or critically, "to correct their notebooks, or to give them good, average, or bad marks."[94]

In addition, along with Barth, Cullmann, and Hendrik Berkhof, Ellul thinks that, on the one hand, the "powers" do indeed have an objective, authentic, spiritual reality.[95] On the other hand, he suggests that the "powers" do not act in total independence, but only in relation with man. That is, "they find expression in human, social realities, in the enterprise of man."[96] They are "incarnated in very concrete forms, and this power is expressed in institutions or organizations."[97]

Thus, for Ellul, almost anything could be a "power:" law, sex, technology, state, religion, science, the city, and so on. Money, to take one example to which he has devoted an entire book, can be a power. Money, Ellul argues, has an attraction,

---

[93] See Gill's "Jacques Ellul's View of Scripture," pp. 472-473.

[94] Karl Barth, Evangelical Theology, An Introduction, trans. by Grover Foley (Grand Rapids: Eerdmans, 1980), p. 31.

[95] See Gill's The Word of God in the Ethics of Jacques Ellul, p. 124, n. 56. We should mention here that Ellul interprets that stoichea as the basic elements of the world, particularly the human social structures which are "transposed into force, activity, and seduction by the intervention of a power" (The Ethics of Freedom, p. 154). Thus, while the stoichea are closely related to the exousiai, the two are not synonymous.

[96] Ellul, The Ethics of Freedom, p. 152.

[97] Idem, Violence, p. 163. In his book Money and Power (pp. 75-76), Ellul writes that "power is something that acts by itself, is capable of moving other things, is autonomous (or claims to be), is a law unto itself, and presents itself as an active agent. This is its first characteristic. Its second is that power has a spiritual value. It is not only of the material world, although this is where it acts. It has spiritual meaning and direction...Finally, power is more or less personal."

power and value which far exceed its economic function. Jesus compared it to a god. This was no mere rhetorical device on His part. How else can one explain not only rampant avarice, but the fact that whole societies are structured around money? Marx was right to show how money involves a "mechanism of naked power" which alienates us all.[98]

Nuclear development offers another illustration. One reason Ellul warns against unlimited nuclear proliferation is its link with "the spirit of unbridled power." Power is not, he writes, as past theologians have mistakenly thought, a mere psychological defect of the individual. According to the Bible, the powers "overcome us and make us act; they are existential and collective impulses."[99] The spiritual, material and human factors, then, all coalesce in Ellul's definition of the "powers."

Ironically, God chose the path of non-power to defeat the "powers." Through the incarnation, God voluntarily divested himself of his omnipotence and became a man. In His crucifixion and resurrection, Jesus Christ freely chose the path of non-power in order to liberate humanity.[100] The crucifixion was not the tragic and unforeseen end of a frustrated apocalyptic leader, the final victory of the political powers of the day (cf. Schweitzer). Jesus willingly chose the path of non-power. Through his death and resurrection, the "powers" have already and objectively been despoiled (Colossians 2:14). While the powers are defeated, this does not mean that they are entirely eliminated, for the creation still awaits the Not Yet of God's kingdom. Scripture tells us, though, according to Ellul, that in the end the powers are finally damned and annihilated. They do not, per Barth and Cullmann, have any possible participation in redemption. Their doom, which has been secured in Jesus Christ, is sure and certain.[101]

---

[98]Idem, The Ethics of Freedom, p. 154.

[99]Idem, "Unbridled Spirit of Power," Sojourners 11.7 (July--August 1982): 14.

[100]Idem, "La Croix et la liberté," p. 6. Power, according to Ellul, "is always violent, unjust, and [the] creator of victims" (ibid). A constant theme of his The Ethics of Freedom, he writes, is "the incompatability between freedom and power" (p. 12).

[101]See Apocalypse, pp. 201-213, "Damnation of the Powers," and Gill, The Word of God in the Ethics of Jacques Ellul, p. 109.

2. The subjective/internal

Christ frees the believer not only from the external constraints of the effects of necessity, and from the influence of the "powers," but also from the subjective/inward self and from the personal bondage of sin characterized by the "flesh." "As God enters into human life, it isn't only the exterior bondages which he destroys, it is also our own bondage from ourselves."[102]

The biblical idea of the "flesh," according to Ellul, connotates four ideas, all of which overlap and are the object of Christ's liberation. In a neutral sense, our flesh is what separates us from God. It is our finitude or our creaturelikeness. We all encounter the finitude imposed by space and time. People are born, grow, and die.[103] In itself, this is not an evil, of course, nor exactly the object of our liberation, except possibly in some eschatological sense. Yet our finitude, Ellul suggests, is also something sinful man always tries to transcend, and in this sense it can lead to evil. The failure to accept and to come to grips with one's finitude leads to all sorts of perverted freedoms. Refusing to accept the limitations of nature, for example, man exploits nature in the name of freedom.

Secondly, and related to this, a person's finitude issues forth in a spirit of power which results in "an expression of weakness and of fear of nothingness."[104] This, in turn, becomes the source of covetousness and man's spirit of domination. Third, Ellul contends that the "flesh" represents "the power of man in his opposition to God,"[105] seen in Scripture, for example, in the contrast between the works of the Spirit and the works of the flesh (Galatians 5). Last, the "flesh" denotes man's anxiety, self-centeredness, pride and egocentricity. This expresses itself in man's constant fears regarding self-importance, his fear of insignificance, his apprehension about his

---

[102]Ellul, "La Croix et la liberté," p. 5.

[103]Idem, "La Responsabilité du christianisme dans la nature et la liberté," Combat Nature 54 (January-February 1983): 17.

[104]Idem, The Ethics of Freedom, p. 134.

[105]Ibid.

guilty past and his uncertain future, and anxiety about what Ellul calls "the work of my hands."[106]

The liberation from the "flesh" in Jesus Christ, then, constitutes not so much the gift of self-determination, the mere ability to make choices (although it does not exclude this), but rather a determination of the self through conversion and regeneration. Through what Ellul calls an "incredible reversal" at "the very root of our being,"[107] the Holy Spirit usurps the role which the "flesh" once played (cf. Galatians 2:20). Indwelt by Christ and led by the Spirit, the Christian's life is characterized by freedom in relation to the self (2 Corinthians 3:16). Granted, the final effects of this liberation are Not Yet, and the fruits of the Spirit are often limited and indecisive (Romans 7). Yet, writes Ellul, "the freedom which we are given encompasses the whole complex of the flesh: the power which is against God, covetousness-impotence, the spirit of might and conquest, and the simple boundary and finitude which is a reminder of man's distinction from God."[108]

E. Freedom-For

Freedom given by God in Jesus Christ defines the Christian life. For Ellul, freedom is not one virtue among others, or one aspect of the Christian life. According to him, the biblical message, and particularly the Apostle Paul, go much further: "La liberté ne fait pas partie de la vie chrétienne, elle 'est' la vie chrétienne tout entière."[109] In short, without freedom there is no Christian life.

This is not all. This freedom given in Christ and which constitutes the <u>sine qua non</u> of the Christian life knows no boundaries. It is "alive, unlimited, without restrictions or obligations. It enables us to throw off all constraints and admonitions."[110] Four times, Ellul points out, the Apostle Paul tells us that "all things are lawful." Any lifestyle, any

---

[106]See Ellul's article, "Work and Calling."

[107]Idem, "Le Sens," p. 8.

[108]Idem, The Ethics of Freedom, p. 135.

[109]Idem, "Le Sens," p. 6.

[110]Idem, The Ethics of Freedom, p. 186. Cf. "Le Sens," p. 9: "It is necessary to persuade ourselves that there are no limits to this freedom."

political persuasion, any Christian way of life is possible. This, we recall, is one of the reasons freedom is so hard to define. It can assume an infinite variety of differing forms. The Church, unfortunately, has never been comfortable with this message which sounds so antinomian, says Ellul. This explains its unfortunate but deserved reputation for moralizing, for preserving the status quo through authoritarian and imperialistic means and ethical legislation. This lost message must be rediscovered and proclaimed anew, writes Ellul, for this is the Church's most urgent task.[111]

This absolute and unrestricted freedom is not without a specific orientation, however. It has certain consequences that one must also understand. Any failure to grasp these consequences means that one has not understood the true nature of Christian freedom, and that one has lapsed back into a mistaken idea, such as that freedom means mere independence or autonomy, the lack of restraints, the opportunity to do anything at all. Examples of this abound. In one article, Ellul gives the example of the Christian abuse of nature. The argument is simple: liberated by God concerning everything, man becomes master over all. This is compounded by the fact that Christianity "individualizes to the extreme," making the single individual more important than any social group. The tragic result, then, is the exploitation and degradation of nature.[112]

Such an outcome represents a tragic and unbearable abuse of freedom, according to Ellul. While the freedom in Christ is total, it is not unspecific, vague, without direction or significance.[113] Ellul suggests that Christian freedom has what he calls "a double orientation," consisting of love of neighbor and the glory of God.[114] This "but" is not a limitation or a restriction. Ellul contends that he is not taking away with his left hand what he has just given with the right. He is merely showing the implications and direction of freedom. If freedom is truly authentic, he says, it must be both expedient (l'utilité) and edifying (l'édification).[115] Just as Paul wrote that all things are lawful, he also wrote

---

[111] Ibid., p. 193.

[112] Idem, "La Responsabilité du christianisme dans la nature et la liberté," p. 16.

[113] Idem, "Le Sens," p. 10.

[114] Ibid., p. 18.

[115] Ibid., p. 11.

that not all things edified, and that he took great pains to bring his body under subjection. What, exactly, does Ellul mean by love and the glory of God?

1. God's glory

God's glory is not a Feuerbachian projection of human qualities raised to their highest degree. Nor does glorifying God consist of repeating special words or singing certain songs. God's glory, writes Ellul, is "his general revelation to the eyes of men of all that he is,"[116] or "in other words, God's glory is his revelation, both general and particular, to the eyes of men. It is the revelation of God as he is, or as he gives himself to be known."[117] Thus, to glorify God means to reflect his true nature to others in the way we live, to reveal his will, which is love, patience and availability, in all our actions and decisions. Without this first orientation, a "vertical" relation to God's glory, freedom is totally without meaning or value.[118] At every step of the way, Christian freedom must reflect the true nature and will of God.

2. Love of neighbor

The second orientation of freedom, inseparable from the first, is the "horizontal" orientation of love. In two places Ellul writes that love and freedom are the two poles of the Christian life, and that the totality of the Christian life exists as a dialectical movement between the two poles.[119] In good dialectical fashion, he tells us that neither pole can exist alone. Just as freedom without regard for the glory of God is vacuous, even so there is no freedom without love. Only actions done in love are truly free, and to destroy one pole is

---

[116] Ibid., p. 14. On God's glory, see pages 13-16 of this article.

[117] Idem, The Ethics of Freedom, p. 214. Ellul discusses God's glory on pages 213-219 of this book. Although it certainly sounds like it, I am not at all certain that in the last two references Ellul is affirming natural theology. He is far too much of a Barthian, despite his criticisms, to do that.

[118] Idem, "Le Sens," p. 19.

[119] See "Le Sens," p. 7, and The Ethics of Freedom, p. 206.

to destroy the other.[120] Ellul's explication of the nature of love is hardly new or creative, and we need not complicate his point. To love means, quite simply, to exist as a neighbor for my fellow human being, to place his interests above my own, and not to scandalize him if he is a weaker brother. Love means to choose that which will profit and edify another.[121]

3. Application and conclusion

To recall a previously mentioned example, that of man's relation to nature and the environment, how do love and the glory of God provide a specific orientation for freedom? Ellul suggests three "very simple lessons."[122] First, God entrusted the creation to man, not so that he could despoil and exploit it for his own selfish use, but so that he could manage it in the name of God. That is, man was to "behave as God toward creation." All of his actions in relation to nature should thus reflect the nature and will of God. Thus, as God's vice-regent, man must oversee nature "not only for blind and egotistical profit but by love." He bears this responsibility and must answer for it. Freedom which does not acknowledge this is not a true liberation, but a radical perversion.

Secondly, man must also acknowledge his limitations. According to Ellul, this requires an acceptance and understanding of one's finitude, and the finitude, in this instance, of the earth's resources. Man must acknowledge what Ellul calls "thresholds," the points at which our actions have the opposite effect of their intention (he gives the example of wrongly administered medicine which makes a person more ill). In addition, man must voluntarily choose to limit his choices. This, writes Ellul, "is the supreme expression of freedom."

Third, Ellul suggests that a proper relation to nature requires the use of "power voluntarily limited." Jesus perfectly

---

[120]See "La Croix et la liberté," p. 6; "L'Antidestin," p. 9; and The Ethics of Freedom, p. 200.

[121]Ellul, "Le Sens," pp. 12-13. On Ellul's idea of love, see Outka in JE:IE (pp. 197-203, and 218-222). Outka characterizes Ellul's concept of love as "personalistic," for it stresses interindividual relationships over social ones, and as placing an infinite value on each person.

[122]What follows is a brief summary of part of Ellul's article, "La Responsabilité du christianisme dans la nature et liberté."

exemplifies this in his choice of the path of non-power. Elsewhere Ellul refers to this as the absolute rejection of the spirit of domination, of Eros, which is but a will to power, in favor of Agape.[123]

In conclusion, then, "freedom-for" is hardly an easy thing. It is not a simple matter to live out freedom. In fact, Ellul describes it as a "difficult adventure" or a "risk,"[124] a "burden" which calls us to responsibility and accountability.[125] Freedom, according to Ellul, is a fragile thing. We can squander it. In many instances, although people say they want freedom, in reality, they are quite unwilling to assume it. Man does not want to confront himself; he does not really want to be free. He prefers what Ellul calls his "beloved chains" (chaînes adorées).[126] People fear it, preferring comfort and security to the risk, invention and creativity which freedom requires. It is impossible, however, writes Ellul, to have one's cake and to eat it too, "to claim to be free in a world of laws and security."[127] Far from granting mere autonomy or independence, a life void of direction or order, freedom has a concrete orientation and specificity: "If we live in love and for glory [of God] we are in freedom; otherwise freedom does not exist."[128]

F. Conclusion

In concluding this chapter on Ellul's idea of freedom, we can make two observations. First, we see here, as elsewhere, his radically christocentric method: apart from Jesus Christ there simply is no true freedom. In Ellul's thought, Christ is both the only source and the perfect paradigm of liberation.

---

[123]See "La Croix et la liberté," p. 6; The Ethics of Freedom, p,. 200, n. 6; and Betrayal, pp. 71-81. Ellul says that he has no problem at all in affirming the well-known distinctions made by Nygren on these terms.

[124]Ellul, "La Peur de la liberté," p. 5.

[125]Idem, "Le Sens," p. 16. Cf. "La Croix et la liberté," p. 6.

[126]Idem, "La Blancheur de la liberté," Réforme 1525 (June 8, 1974): 3.

[127]Idem, "La Peur de la liberté," p. 5.

[128]Idem, "Le Sens," p. 18.

Ellul uses this same christological method in many places in his work, and it need not surprise us here. In his work <u>The Theo-logical Foundation of Law</u>, for example, he insists upon the radical necessity of divine revelation, and on the idea that Jesus Christ embodies and unites all the characteristics of God's righteousness. Apart from Christ, he argues, there is no justice, not even a relative justice, and no human law. The foundation, realization, and qualifications of human law reside in him alone.[129]

So it is here. Human freedom becomes a real possibility only to the extent to which it is founded in the perfect freedom of God, given in Christ and witnessed to in Holy Scripture.[130] Christians alone can be free, and they serve the world with a special vocation: they are "called upon as bearers of freedom in this society; bearers of freedom when technological condi-tioning is getting more and more rigorous, more and more determining for people."[131] Ellul encounters heavy criticism for such exclusivity. Two observations, though, put his position in perspective.

First, he distinguishes between salvation and freedom. While the former can exist without the latter, the converse is not true. Christian freedom is not a predisposed privilege dropped down from heaven. Rather, it imposes the heaviest burden imaginable upon people, one which many people do not want. It is, then, not a cause for pride or condescension but for humility.

Second, Ellul does seem to indicate that efforts or move-ments of freedom apart from the Christian revelation can at least be partially effective. They are possible as a sort of by-product of the objective work of Christ, and are not to be discounted.[132] Ellul's own involvement with delinquent juveniles for nearly 30 years illustrates this point. While the kids may never come to a mature Christian freedom in Jesus Christ, they can indeed be helped to become what Ellul calls "positively maladjusted."[133]

---

[129] Idem, The Theological Foundation of Law, pp. 42-44.

[130] On the absoluteness and exclusivity of the Gospel, see Apocalypse, pp. 106-107, and 110.

[131] Ellul, POOA, p. 110.

[132] Idem, "L'Antidestin," p. 122.

[133] Idem, "Les Marges de la liberté en Occident," pp. 1-2.

Our second concluding observation constitutes a summary categorization of Ellul's idea of freedom. It is what I would call "synergistic." That is, freedom, for him, requires the co-operative interaction of two discrete agencies, God and man. According to Ellul, God never acts without man. He loves man, "hence he never regards him as a mere object. He respects man. Hence he never acts on him from outside."[134] It is equally true, though, he goes on to say in this passage, that freedom does not depend only on man. There is an objective reality which is given in Jesus Christ. Elsewhere Ellul has called this the "twofold movement" of man's obedience and God's free grace.

The life of Jonah exemplifies this. His story "brings out a remarkable aspect of the strategy which God patiently follows in the world."[135] Chosen by God to be his instrument of grace, Jonah nevertheless flees. God's strategy, however, is not to damn him, to reject, coerce, or force Jonah as a _deus ex machina_. No, his strategy is "infinitely more subtle and complex" than we might imagine.[136] He respects Jonah's decisions and yet in the end Jonah fulfills his will almost "in spite of himself."[137]

Freedom, according to Ellul, requires this dynamic interaction between God and man. It is not something which is static, but is dynamic and personal. While this "yes and no" response of Ellul will certainly frustrate many, especially with its explicit affirmation of two things which appear to contradict each other from the human perspective, his goal is to do justice to what he feels is the message of the biblical text. On the objective level, God's gracious gift of freedom in Jesus Christ is his alone to give. On the subjective level, however, it is not something magically bestowed, but something which requires the faith and response of the believer.

---

[134] Idem, _The Ethics of Freedom_, p. 78.

[135] Idem, _The Judgement of Jonah_, p. 32.

[136] Ibid., p. 33.

[137] Ibid., p. 35. Compare _The Politics of God and the Politics of Man_, p. 57, and _Living Faith_, p. 257.

CHAPTER FIVE

ELLUL'S THEOLOGICAL METHOD: A REVIEW AND PROSPECT

If Ellul cannot have a large following fully faithful to his
thought, he does merit a readership that will confront and argue
with him and his vision. I use "confront" advisedly, and am not
alone among the writers of these pages who do so. One engages
the thought of Ellul; there is no such thing as a casual reading
followed by mild acceptance or bland rejection. In his writing
there is much of the spirit that says, in effect, "Eat, bird, or
die."

Martin Marty
"Creative Misuses of Jacques Ellul"[1]

A. Introduction

Ellul has always had and will continue to have both ardent
followers and vehement detractors. His writings, in both their
content and style, are far too controversial to permit any sort
of neutrality. People tend to love him or hate him, and not
without reason. Ellul brooks no waffling compromise and does
not balk at making stringent judgements against those with whom
he disagrees. The purpose of this chapter is to review the
previous ones and to engage Ellul on a critical level so as to
evaluate his theological method.

In some ways Ellul's theological method does not proffer
anything novel. He writes out of a distinct confessional
stance, the Reformed Church of France. He explicitly acknowledges the marked influence which Barth has had on his thought,
sees his own work as a sort of extension of Barth, and expresses
amazement at those who think the theology of the Swiss giant is
no longer serviceable for contemporary theology. While it may
be true that contemporary theology's agenda as regards its
methodology is in chaos,[2] a lamentation expressed by every new
generation it seems, Ellul offers no major departures for a
positive biblical theology. Unlike Kaufman, he suggests no need
for a radical reconception or reconstruction in theological

---

[1]Marty, pp. 3-4.

[2]For several examples of this dismay see Kaufman's An
Essay on Theological Method (pp. ix-x), Thomas Altizer's forward
to Mark Taylor's Deconstructing Theology (p. xi), and John
Cobb's Living Options in Protestant Theology (pp. 8, 323).

method.[3]   We   may   venture   to   say   that   he   would   dismiss
Kaufman's proposal for theology as "imaginative construction" as
altogether   superficial   and   as   an   excellent   example   of what
Feuerbach had in mind when he wrote his <u>The Essence of Christi-
anity</u>.   Even   less   would   Ellul   endorse   Taylor's   more recent
proposal for   "deconstruction."[4]   Theologians   who   are   looking
for   methodological   novelty   will   be   sadly   disappointed   with
Ellul's enterprise.

On the other hand, though, Ellul brings to the theological
task a creativity and freshness which tends to shed new light on
old problems and invest the theological task with new vigor.   If
he   would   altogether   disapprove   of   the novelty of Kaufman and
Taylor, this does not mean he thinks it is sufficient to restate
old formulas.   He would criticize just as severely, I think,
Thomas Oden's <u>Agenda for Theology</u>, which proposes a theological
reform "in the direction of antiquity."[5]   Although he would
agree with Oden's criticism of modernity's "exaltation of the
<u>modo</u>,"[6]   or   what   C.S.   Lewis   once   called   modern   man's
inclination to chronological snobbery, he would find it totally
insufficient simply to restate any supposed ecumenical orthodoxy
or <u>consensus</u> <u>fidelium</u> which claims the   support of a (dubious)
Vincentian canon (<u>quod</u> <u>ubique</u>,   <u>quod</u> <u>semper</u>, <u>quod</u> <u>ab</u> <u>omnibus</u>
<u>creditum</u> <u>est</u>).   Ellul has far too much historical sensitivity
for   such   a program.   We have seen, for example, how he restates
the work of Christ in the more modern terms of liberation.
Likewise, to take another example, when constructing his own
Christian ethic, Ellul insists that any simple restatement of
the   ethical   insights   of   Augustine,   Ambrose, Calvin or Luther
overlooks the obvious point that their social, political, and
economic   setting   was   so   different   from   ours   that   "their
conclusions (if not their point of departure and their method)
are thus entirely outmoded."[7]

Thus, in some ways Ellul's theological method proffers
nothing at all novel.   In other ways, though, part of his
brilliance is his ability to match his commitment to a positive

---

[3]Kaufman, pp. 18, footnote #10; 26, and 30.

[4]Mark   Taylor,   <u>Deconstructing   Theology</u>   (New   York: The
Crossroad Publishing Company and Scholars Press, 1982).

[5]Thomas   Oden,   <u>Agenda   for   Theology</u> (San Francisco: Harper
and Row, 1979), p. 11.

[6]Ibid., p. 27.

[7]Ellul, <u>To Will and to Do</u>, p. 225.

biblical theology with an intense desire to make theology practical and relevant. Unlike Kaufman, Taylor or Oden, Ellul would take seriously the suggestion made by Cobb that theology must have real interests in both the Bible and modern culture.[8] He attempts to steer something of a middle course between critical/liberal theology and fundamentalistic orthodoxy. He readily accepts the advancements of critical scholarship wherever he finds them valid, and incorporates them into his own theological framework.[9]

Although we can expect several additions to his corpus in the near future,[10] there is no question but that the bulk of his contribution to theology has been made. We may proceed, then, with our critique with a tentative assurance, not entirely warranted in previous years, that our conclusions have the broad support of most of his corpus.

The course of this chapter is as follows: After a brief review of the first four chapters and the conclusions drawn from them, we shall propose both some weaknesses and some strengths of Ellul's theological method. We may state the general tenor of the following critique in this way. We reject the wholesale acceptance of Ellul, exemplified, for instance, in Matheke's work, where there is no substantial criticism of Ellul at all. In addition to being unrealistic, this approach betrays the very spirit of Ellul, who challenges his readers to engage his thought and to do better. Even the conclusion of Fasching's excellent work seems to be a bit too strong, that "Ellul's contribution to contemporary theology is monumental. His work

---

[8] Cobb, p. 11.

[9] Another recent attempt to use Barth's theology as a paradigm for an evangelical theology is Bernard Ramm's After Fundamentalism: The Future of Evangelical Theology (New York: Harper and Row, 1983). Ramm writes that his "essay in theological methodology" has four major themes: (1) the Enlightenment shattered orthodox theology, which has yet to recover from the blow; (2) neither liberalism nor orthodoxy has met the challenges of the Enlightenment; (3) Barth represents the most successful attempt to date to meet this challenge; and (4) Barth therefore offers evangelicals a paradigm or model by which to do theology.

[10] In addition to his two-volume autobiography, which has been written but which will not be published until after his death, Ellul is currently at work on a commentary on Ecclesiastes and The Ethics of Holiness, which is the second installment of his proposed three-part ethic.

is a comprehensive _tour de force_."[11] Instead, we will aim for what Edward Long referred to as the "judiciously cautious loyalty" of Gill's work.[12] Like Gill, we see both promise and problems in Ellul. Theologians will by all means benefit by going through Ellul, but they must also go beyond him.[13]

B. Review and Conclusions

Chapter One attempted to describe and analyze, by means of a typology, four major perspectives from which to view Ellul's method, and to evaluate the current status of the Ellul literature. We saw that there are good and valid reasons to read Ellul as a theological positivist, an existential thinker, a prophet and a dialectician. He is in some ways all of these and not one of them exclusively. Readers need to make careful distinctions, however, when applying these types to Ellul. He is not a rock-ribbed Calvinist nor an uncompromising Barthian. He has never been a Catholic. He has no formal allegiance to the philosophical school of existentialism. Ellul is far too independent in his thinking to fit in mechanically with any one of the types. In light of this first chapter we can make two conclusions.

First, if sheer quantity of literature about a person is any indicator of his or her importance, Ellul ranks as one of contemporary theology's giants. His own corpus exceeds 40 books and 800 articles, and it continues to grow. Joyce Hanks has documented over 1100 secondary works about Ellul and is in the process of supplementing her bibliography. Thus, Edward Long simply erred, as many have on this matter, when he wrote recently (1984) that "the interpretive literature about Jacques Ellul available to the American reader is relatively modest."[14] While much of the secondary literature on Ellul is not always accurate or dependable, a handful of scholars such as Eller, Fasching, Gill, Hanks and Vahanian have engaged Ellul's thought and interacted on a meaningful level with his program. Thus, with Hanks' bibliography, and with a careful eye for separating

---

[11] Fasching, _The Thought of Jacques Ellul_, p. 177.

[12] Edward Long, "Forward" to Gill's _The Word of God in the Ethics of Jacques Ellul_, p. xi.

[13] I am deliberately using the language of the title of Gill's last chapter here.

[14] Long, p. ix.

the wheat from the chaff in the secondary literature, true bibliographic control in Ellul research is now possible.

We have already hinted at our second conclusion from Chapter One, which is that although Ellul writes from a definite theological perspective, he is an academic generalist with eclectic interests and abilities. Equally at home in law, history, sociology and biblical exegesis, the breadth and depth of Ellul's scholarship is far-ranging. This aspect of his work has several related consequences. It explains both his broad appeal to different groups and the offense which specialists take when Ellul transgresses their sacred domains with what they perceive as reckless abandon. Further, Ellul's eclectic interests make it most difficult to pigeonhole him, which in his case is a risky business anyway. He draws upon the insights of Barth, Kierkegaard, and Marx, thinkers whom he acknowledges as his benefactors, but he harbors nothing like an unswerving allegiance to any of them. Ellul is more than willing to criticize them at any point he feels is necessary.

A simple example illustrates this second conclusion. If we take Niebuhr's typology found in <u>Christ and Culture</u>, where does Ellul fit in? Many put him in the first category, of Christ against culture. There are good reasons for this. Ellul presents a radical critique of modern culture and its values. He stresses the absolute and sole authority of Jesus Christ and the necessity of the Christian's radical obedience to Him. Yet Ellul is anything but a legalist. He would abhor any withdrawal from culture. In addition, his vigorous affirmation of universalism would hardly fit in here.

What about the Christ of culture? This category probably applies least to Ellul, but even here we can observe some affinities on his part with the type. He certainly has what Neibuhr calls a "this-worldly concern." Ellul would affirm many of the concerns of a Rauschenbusch (one of Niebuhr's examples for this type), such as the plight of the poor, the nature and reality of social evil, the oppressive effect of corporations and governments, and so forth. On the other hand, he would reject many of the presuppositions of the liberal theology which best exemplifies this type. Likewise, although he would hardly agree with any synthesis of Christ and culture, typical of the Christ above culture type and exemplified by Aquinas, Ellul does have a similar concern that the two realms be directly related. The Christian has no choice but to take both at once.

Perhaps Ellul fits in best with Niebuhr's fourth type, the dualist perspective of Christ and culture in paradox illustrated by Luther.[15] His Christocentricity, existential leanings, and his "double attitude"[16] as a "dynamic, dialectical thinker"[17] all coincide with this type. For Ellul, as for the dualist, life is both tragic and joyful, and the final solution to the problem of Christ and culture lies beyond history or death. For now the Christian lives between the times.[18] Yet Ellul departs from this type at strategic points. His universalism dissolves the tension between divine wrath and mercy which the true dualist would maintain. One would also be hardpressed to label Ellul a cultural or political conservative.[19]

Ellul could also affirm many of the points found in the conversionist type whereby Christ transforms culture. He clearly affirms that God acts in history, that man's responses to these acts are crucial, that the gospel ushers in a presence of the future kingdom today, and, to take Niebuhr's example of F.D. Maurice, that God's love results in the salvation of all people.[20] Whether Ellul has a "more positive and hopeful attitude toward culture" than the dualist, though, is doubtful. [21]

This brief excursus on Niebuhr's typology helps to illustrate our second conclusion, that Ellul is a generalist with eclectic interests and expertise, and that his interpreters need to take care in labeling him. Coupled with our first conclusion about the immense amount of primary and secondary literature on and by Ellul, we can mention a practical implication before

---

[15]One particular passage from Niebuhr seems to apply to Ellul especially well: "The dualist lives in conflict, and in the presence of one great issue. That conflict is between God and man, or better--since the dualist is an existential thinker--between God and us...[His] logical starting point in dealing with the cultural problem is the great act of reconciliation and forgiveness that has occurred in the divine-human battle--the act we call Jesus Christ." See H. Richard Niebuhr, <u>Christ and Culture</u> (New York: Harper Torchbooks, 1951), p. 150.

[16]Niebuhr, p. 171.

[17]Ibid., p. 179.

[18]Ibid., pp. 178, 185.

[19]Ibid., p. 159.

[20]Ibid., pp. 195, 225-227.

[21]Ibid., p. 191.

moving on to a review of Chapter Two. The practical result of these first two conclusions is that it is necessary to read broadly in Ellul's corpus in order to understand his project. Sampling bits and pieces of Ellul or the secondary literature about him is almost certain to result in truncated views about him.

In Chapter Two we narrowed our perspective and focused on Ellul as a dialectician, concluding that although he has eclectic interests, the operative assumption which undergirds all he writes is his commitment to a dialectical method. In the words of Gill, this specific commitment to dialectic is the "one characteristic which permeates every thought and every analysis rendered by Jacques Ellul."[22]

Ellul's own dialectical method follows in the tradition of that historical movement in theology which Barth, Brunner, Bultmann, Thurneysen, and Gogarten pioneered in the early decades of this century. It has more distant roots in the dialectic of Kierkegaard, which broke with the 19th century emphasis on the continuity of all life and instead stressed discontinuity. The ultimate source of Ellul's commitment to dialectic, though, rests in his conviction that the Bible itself contains and exemplifies true dialectic. We went on to suggest in Chapter Two that Ellul's dialectic operates on three interrelated levels. He uses dialectic to describe the nature of reality or the real life phenomena, as an epistemological tool to interpret and understand this reality, and as a theological method by which to interpret Scripture and to describe a Christian mode of existence.

Perhaps the most important conclusion of this second chapter for theological method lies in Ellul's commitment to hold his theological and socio-historical works in tension. That is, he is convinced that the right relationship between these two fields is one of dialectical tension, correlation, confrontation and criticism. Sociology forces theology to be timely, relevant, concrete and self-critical. This helps to eliminate some of the other-worldly tendencies of a strong positive Biblical theology. Theology, on the other hand, challenges sociology to be more wholistic and criticizes its value assumptions which tend to be reductionistic (such as that man is defined solely in terms of his work or his economic production). Theology brings to bear the revelation of God's Word on the findings of the social sciences. We saw how Ellul's corpus, with books written in each of these two disciplines,

---

[22]Gill, The Word of God in the Ethics of Jacques Ellul, p. 157.

illustrates this dialectical relationship between theology and sociology.

Chapters Three and Four narrowed our purview even further by suggesting an original interpretive key to Ellul's work. At this point we moved from descriptive analysis (Chapters One and Two) to a more interpretive or synthetic perspective. We showed how the one dialectic between freedom and necessity runs as a golden thread throughout all of his books. Without suggesting that this is the only important factor in his method, which would be reductionistic, we simply attempted to try to locate in his own method something like what he tries to find in his analysis of society, that is, a constituent element or main idea.

Necessity constitutes the first pole of this dialectic. Disclaiming any of the metaphysical overtones which this word has, Ellul writes that all people everywhere act as though they were free, and continually strive after freedom, but nevertheless struggle with some sense of destiny, fate or necessity (all of which Ellul uses as synonymous in this context).[23] The origin for this order of necessity, according to Ellul, resides in the Fall which we read about in Genesis and which Ellul interprets in a conservative and traditional way. Prior to the Fall, humankind's relationship with God was characterized by intimate love, spontaneity and freedom. The Fall, however, brought about a move "from the realm of freedom into the realm of necessity."[24] This enslavement to sin and necessity constitutes the origin of and embraces all the manifold sociological determinisms about which Ellul writes. Cultural sclerosis, entropy, static conformity and uniformity, and the total lack of any truly revolutionary possibilities are only forms or expressions of the basic theological cleavage which took place in Genesis.[25] We went on to illustrate how this order of necessity emerges in both the church and in society in general (technique, propaganda and politics).

Freedom constitutes the positive pole of this dialectic. In Chapter Four, after disabusing ourselves of what Ellul would call illusions and misconceptions of freedom, we went on to describe the source, object and orientation of freedom. Based in the pure freedom of God, who alone is fully free, incarnated in Jesus Christ as witnessed to in Holy Scripture, freedom is

---

[23] Ellul, "L'Antidestin."

[24] Idem, "Technique and the Opening Chapters of Genesis," p. 134.

[25] Idem, "Le Sens," p. 4.

offered to all people. All of Scripture, and the Apostle Paul in particular, witness to the reality that God reveals Himself first, foremost and always as the liberator. He frees people from the external/objective exousia and the effects of necessity, and from the internal/subjective enslavement to the sinful flesh. While Christian freedom, according to Ellul, is absolute and without limits, it is not without the concrete orientation of God's glory and the love of neighbor. Available to all, this freedom is found exclusively in Jesus Christ and nowhere else.

Having reviewed our broad conclusions in the analytic description of Ellul as an eclectic (Chapter One) and a dialectician (Chapter Two), and in the synthesis and interpretation that the key to his dialectic thought rests in the dialectic of freedom and necessity (Chapters Three and Four), we are now in a position to proffer a critical evaluation of Ellul's theological method. In what follows we shall present four weaknesses and three strengths, aiming for what we cited above as a "judiciously cautious loyalty" to Ellul's project. Our criticisms, we should note, all center around the matter of Ellul's own consistency with his professed dialectical method. In other words, my criticisms are "internal" ones, as Cobb puts it, for they all have to do with Ellul's "avowed starting point and procedure [of dialectic] and the actual performance."[26] I will show that Ellul's works contain some definite unilateral or non-dialectical tendencies which depart from his avowed method.

C. Dialectic Betrayed

1. Rhetoric and the loss of dialogue

Anyone who has read only a little of Ellul can attest to one of the most salient features of his writing, his impassioned rhetoric or what Martin Marty calls the "absolutist character" of his thought.[27] Instead of engaging his reader, this trait can sometimes have the opposite and unintentional effect of alienating and distancing him or her. Ellul's impassioned rhetoric can cut off any dialectic of dialogue before it even begins. Ellul does his own cause a greater disservice, it seems, for he loses many people who might otherwise engage his thought and dialogue with his ideas. Although he would most certainly deny it, the feeling one gets from reading Ellul is that he is right and all who disagree with him are wrong. The last thing Ellul wants, his rhetoric seems to indicate, is a

---

[26]Cobb, p. 312.

[27]Marty, p. 7.

dialectical exchange of ideas. Ellul specializes in the absolutist monologue.

Some of his language is what we could call confusing and imprecise. We have seen how he continually disclaims any interest in what he calls "metaphysical" problems, which for him is a pejorative word. He repeatedly denies that his idea of necessity means anything like mechanistic causality, yet he continues to use words which are freighted with emotional baggage: l'insurmontable, un destin implacable, fatum, détermin-isme, mécanisme de détermination, nécessité, ananké, and the like.[28] Ellul almost never defines these words in anything like a formal way and the reader is left to fend for himself in determining just what Ellul means. We can well imagine that the words which we have just cited would raise red flags in the minds of many of his readers.

In addition to this unclear use of language, much of Ellul's rhetoric is simply caustic and inflammatory. He characterizes much of the WCC's work as a tissue of platitudes and errors. The success of Harvey Cox's book The Secular City, he suggests, is hard to understand, with it being "so sociologically and theologically superficial, so ordinary, with its repetition of all the commonplaces about secularization and the profane, and lacking in any depth in the subject...so dubious in its historical analyses and so generalized in its sociology..."[29] Our criticism here is a simple one but not unimportant; and we could easily add scores of other examples. Ellul's use of language is, at times, decidedly non-dialectical. His rhetoric invites antagonism. In his attempt to make his point and to engage his reader he sometimes and inadvertently ends all dialogue before it ever begins.[30]

---

[28]I have taken all of these examples from his article, "L'Antidestin." Compare the first few sentences of To Will and to Do, page 59, for another example of this use of language. I have found only two places where Ellul attempts to clarify his use of language, and those are neither very convincing nor sub-stantial. See Violence (p. 91 note) and The Ethics of Freedom (p. 37).

[29]Ellul, Hope, p. 152. Compare his similar comments on Cox in The Ethics of Freedom, p. 54.

[30]Gill rightly observes that Ellul's use of language is "one of the most difficult to accept aspects" of Ellul's work. See The Word of God in the Ethics of Jacques Ellul, p. 183. Cf. The Meaning of the City, p. xii.

2. Freedom and the reduction of the Christian life

We have seen how for Ellul freedom is not one virtue among many in the Christian life, but rather its sine qua non. Freedom is the one value he holds most dearly and stresses more fervently than any other. It is the supreme goal of all people, he thinks. Our criticism here is that Ellul has construed the Christian life in decidedly monolithic and reductionistic terms which are inconsistent with the richer interplay of various, equally important factors. A more consistently dialectical view of the Christian life would be less unilateral and would give equal or similar emphasis to a variety of factors.

Ellul has, of course, written on other aspects of the Christian life, most notably on faith and hope. His three-part ethic revolves around the Pauline virtues of faith, hope, and love. We should also keep in mind that his emphasis on freedom comes as a result of his analysis of society. That is, he has written about freedom first and most urgently because it is his opinion that it is most lacking and needed today. It is conceivable, in other words, that Ellul could have stressed another aspect of the Christian life if he thought the Sitz im Leben required it. Nevertheless, he has given his readers a partisan and reductionistic vision of the Christian life.

Ellul's tack is not at all unusual. Others have attempted to construe Christianity in terms of a central theme or idea. Käsemann, like Ellul, concentrates on liberation. So do most liberation theologians. Classic liberalism of the 19th century stressed God's benevolent love and the infinite value of the person (cf. Harnack). Schweitzer and the eschatologists draw attention to the primacy of hope, Bultmann to Jesus' radical obedience, orthodox Protestantism to the importance of faith, and so on.[31] The problem for Ellul, though, begins when he argues that freedom is not simply one aspect of the Christian life but that it is the Christian life in toto.

Thus, Ellul appears to be guilty of an overstatement here which denies the more wholistic and dialectical interplay of various factors. Freedom is certainly an important factor in the Christian life, but Ellul offers little support to bolster his claim. He simply states his case about freedom with little more than a superficial statistical argument. Depending on which of his texts we use, Ellul argues that terms relating to freedom occur 50-85 times in the New Testament (he gives no Old Testament figures). A simple check in the concordance reveals

---

[31]Niebuhr makes these observations in Christ and Culture, pp. 15-27.

theological concepts which are, if we use Ellul's type of "proof," far more central to the Christian tradition than freedom. According to Young, terms relating to faith appear 250 times, hope 125 times, and love 350 times in the Bible.[32] Ellul would prove himself more consistent with his avowed dialectical method if he developed more broadly what he hints at in only a few places, that freedom operates dialectically with love and/or hope. His future writings on the ethics of holiness and the ethics of relationship might correct this imbalance, but as for now his unilateral emphasis on freedom presents a reductionistic picture of the Christian life.

3. Power as the enemy of God

Our third criticism of Ellul centers around his thesis concerning the necessary antithesis between freedom and power. According to Ellul, a central theme of his The Ethics of Freedom, is "the incompatability between freedom and power."[33] Power, he writes in another place, is always unjust, violent, domineering and the creator of victims. It is "truly the absolute enemy of God."[34] The crucial problem of power resides in the confluence of the objective structures and entities of power, in what he calls the stoichea in one place (technique, institutions, money, and so on), the exousiai, and the subjective lust for power which all people harbor within themselves. Although some people would have us believe that power is a neutral thing which depends upon its use for its negative or positive value, Ellul disagrees. Power, he says, always tends to run wild. It necessarily corrupts all values which might limit or guide its use. Power always subjugates and subordinates people, and it always tends toward unrestrained growth and the thirst for more power.[35]

The problem of power, then, would appear to be its limitation. Conventional restraints, such as a democratic constitution of checks and balances, a code of ethics, or so forth, all have

---

[32] Robert Young, Analytic Concordance to the Bible, 22nd edition (New York: Funk and Wagnalls, n.d.), pp. 324-325, 490-491, and 622-624.

[33] Ellul, The Ethics of Freedom, p. 12.

[34] Idem, Apocalypse, p. 138.

[35] Idem, "Lust for Power," Katallagete 7.2 (Fall 1979): 30-33.

failed miserably, according to Ellul. An alternative to conventional restraints might be small counter groups which would resist and challenge power. The problem here, though, Ellul says, is that the real powerbrokers would crush such groups, unless these groups fought power with power. Ellul concludes that the one and only alternative to power is the deliberate rejection of power and the unceasing and uncompromising choice of non-power. Our only hope for true freedom rests in this "rejection of all forms of power whatever they may be and no matter how legitimate they are."[36] According to Ellul, Jesus provides the perfect and supreme paradigm of this only way out. In the incarnation, God voluntarily relinquishes his rightful omnipotence in favor of non-power. Ironically, it was through this path of non-power that Jesus defeated the powers.

Ellul is not so much wrong in what he affirms on the relation between power and freedom, but is rather negligent in what he fails to affirm. That is, he is no doubt correct, for example, when he points out that the state has exercised power in totalitarian ways, and that history shows that the state is becoming larger and more influential each year. Yet, it is naive to imagine that the state could ever function as a non-ideological, neutral administrator of the common patrimony. Even if it did or could assume such a non-threatening role, it could not carry it out without the exercise of at least some power.

To take another example, the hegemony of technique has certainly created what Benello has called "unparalleled opportunities for the exercise of power,"[37] and Ellul has done us a service in drawing our attention to its dangers. Technical means of power, control and manipulation have never been greater. Yet, as Ellul admits, we cannot or should not avoid using technique. Yet he never gives us clear guidelines as to a "non-power use" of these "power-full" means. The question is not whether to use power, for we cannot avoid it, but how to use it. Ellul gives us no help here with his rather unrealistic picture.

Ellul would strengthen his argument if he would incorporate the use of power into his dialectic and explain its function from a Christian perspective instead of unilaterally rejecting it. After all, the Gospel to which he is so heartily committed

---

[36] Ibid., p. 33.

[37] C. George Benello, "Technology and Power: Technique as a Mode of Understanding Modernity," in JE:IE, p. 104.

is itself "the power of God unto salvation" (Romans 1:16-17). Ellul seems to have overlooked the fact that the Gospel, which he says is nothing if it is not radically revolutionary in society, is a type of power. Jesus is clear that he came not to bring peace but a sword, division, and strife between people. Time and again He exercised divine power. Likewise, even the adoption and use of non-power by a Christian, to the extent that it is efficacious, constitutes a powerful and disruptive force in society. Indeed, this is its goal, to transform society. We saw in our previous chapters, for example, that one of the tasks of a Christian is to introduce tensions in society, to disrupt the status quo, and to serve as a leavening factor. Ellul never suggests why this is so, how it works out, or in what ways the power of the gospel differs from the other types of power which he so readily rejects.

In one of his most recent books, Stephen Sykes offers an example of a Christian understanding of the use of power. He argues persuasively that the Church finds itself in a situation of chronic and intrinsic conflict, and that this necessarily entails the use of power in conflict resolution. He reviews the Apostle Paul's use of power, examines what he calls one of the few "sociologically-informed" theories of power in the Church (Troeltsch), looks at the theme of power in the New Testament, and then addresses the concrete implications entailed by this necessary use of power by theologians (the primary powerbrokers of the Church, he suggests). According to Sykes, the early Christian community was extremely power-conscious: "to be a Christian was to be equipped with power." It meant one's participation in a community which consisted not of words but of power (1 Corinthians 4:20). Responsible theologians, Sykes concludes, must begin to come to grips with this necessary use of power.[38]

Ellul never comes close to incorporating the use of power into his dialectic. He simply rejects it outright, and this must count as an omission on his part. He would improve his dialectical method and make it more consistent if he would go on to show how power and the exercise of freedom, the latter itself being a type of power, are reciprocally related. Instead, Ellul explains neither the inevitable use of power by all people and institutions, nor the inherent power which partially defines the revolutionary gospel he advocates.

---

[38] Sykes, The Identity of Christianity, Chapter 3, entitled "Power in the Church," pp. 51-77.

4. Universalism and the calm of the lotus

The most glaring inconsistency in Ellul's theological dialectic is his nearly unqualified affirmation of the universal salvation of all people beyond history,[39] a doctrine which Ellul says he accepted as a result of his reading of Barth.[40] As we noted in Chapter Two, some dialectics are what Gurvitch described as "ascending" or Taubes called "synthetic."[41] In Hegel, for example, the dialectic ends in the perfect freedom of the state, while in Marx it ends in the classless, stateless society. For Ellul, the dialectic is similarly ascending or synthetic, for it comes to an end in what he has called "the calm of the lotus."[42] The mode of dialectic, with all its tensions, contradictions and divisions, looks forward to a time of complete peace, balance, unity and calm. Thus, Ellul's dialectic is really only penultimate.

On the one hand, Ellul has continually been charged with fatalism and pessimism. While these charges are understandable and not unwarranted, they must be qualified in light of his universalism. Ellul is a pessimist only on the sociological level. To use his own words: "My purely sociological and historical intellectual approach had led me into a blind alley. There was nothing to say to a person of my society beyond a stoic exhortation to keep going...This concrete situation...was

---

[39] I say "nearly" unqualified because in one place, a footnote, Ellul refers to universalism as an "unfathomable theological problem" which he does not pretend or presume to solve. This, however, seems to me to be a type of false modesty on his part, for the overwhelming weight of all he has written vigorously affirms the doctrine. If the doctrine is latent or implicit in Barth, it is full blown and explicit in Ellul.

[40] Ellul, "Karl Barth and Us," p. 24.

[41] See footnotes #17 and 18 in Chapter Two. Boli-Bennett misses the point, it seems to me, when in his article he implies that Ellul differs from Marx and Hegel because his dialectic does not finally reach a final resolution as it does in the other two thinkers. Universalism does constitute the end of the dialectic or what Ellul called "the calm of the lotus" in his work Humiliation.

[42] Ellul, Humiliation, p. 269. Thus, Menninger is wrong when he writes in his dissertation (p. 190) that Ellul's dialectic never ends. It does end, in the final eschaton beyond history.

fundamentally hopeless."[43]   On the purely sociological level
Ellul acknowledges "the absence of any way out for the world in
which we live, the absence of a prospect for the future."[44]
Without the liberation which God provides in Jesus Christ, "we
can only let ourselves sink into despair...the only solution
left is through a relation with God."[45] This is only on the
sociological level, though, without the theological perspective
of the gospel.

When the counterpoint to the sociological pole is added,
the theological pole, Ellul is, to use to his own words,
"utterly optimistic."[46]   In the end, he adamantly rejects the
idea that people have no hope, that all is lost, and that all we
can do is to sit passively in despair. If Ellul is a qualified
"sociological pessimist," he is most certainly an unqualified
"theological optimist." The reason for this is his conviction
of the truth of universalism:

> So, am I a pessimist? Not at all. I am not pessi-
> mistic because I am convinced that the history of the
> human race, no matter how tragic, will ultimately
> lead to the Kingdom of God. I am convinced that all
> the works of humankind will be reintegrated in the
> work of God, and that each of us, no matter how
> sinful, will ultimately be saved...Consequently, I
> can take the reality we live in very seriously, but
> see it in relation to salvation and God's love, which
> leaves no room for pessimism.[47]

On the sociological level, there is only cause for despair, but
on the theological level, there is only cause for joy and hope.
The hope of the gospel makes the unbearable bearable.[48]

---

[43] Idem, Hope, p. vii.

[44] Ibid., p. 1.

[45] Idem, ISOS, p. 207.   Compare Menninger's dissertation
(p. 218), where in his interview with Ellul, the latter suggests
that apart from Jesus Christ life would be absurd and completely
hopeless, but that with the truth of the gospel this no longer
needs to be the case.

[46] Ibid., p. 82.

[47] Idem, POOA, p. 104.

[48] Idem, Hope, p. 269.   The entire chapter 10 of this book
treats of the relationship between pessimism and optimism.

To bolster his subscription to universalism, beyond his exegetical arguments, Ellul uses at least five theological arguments. First, he distinguishes between judgement and condemnation. The former is only penultimate and never final. It is always positive, revelatory and redemptive, and never retributive or juridical. According to Ellul, we must always view judgement within the context of salvation, for the two are "indissolubly related."[49] Ellul says he has no intention whatsoever of minimizing judgement. He only wants to put it in its rightful perspective. God poured out His final judgement or condemnation on His Son, and to admit that anything less than this is the case is to devalue Christ's work. Jesus Christ bore God's full and final condemnation of sin and evil. Final condemnation, then, is never directed toward people, but only toward the powers.[50]

Second, and closely related to the first point, Ellul emphasizes the priority and triumph of God's love. God loves without limit. His love encompasses all people. He is love even when He judges, "to such a degree that he cannot bear it that his creature should not be finally saved."[51] The entire book of Jonah witnesses to this universally efficacious love of God. This was a hard lesson which Jonah had to learn, that God extends his love even to the ungodly. "As I see it, this position is theologically indisputable: If God is God and if God is love, nothing is outside of the love of God. A place like hell is thus inconceivable. The worst of human beings is still necessarily in the love of God."[52]

A third and minor point which Ellul makes is that we must always keep in mind God's post-deluge promise that He would never again destroy the world in judgement.[53] Fourth, Ellul argues that we should not confuse the exhortations and warnings

---

[49] Idem, The Politics of God and the Politics of Man, p. 76.

[50] On the first point, see The Politics of God and the Politics of Man (pp. 54-56, and 90); ISOS (p. 58); Apocalypse (pp. 65, 112, 123, 158, 172-173, 180, 198, 210, and 213); and Humiliation (pp. 59-60).

[51] Ellul, The Politics of God and the Politics of Man, p. 108.

[52] Idem, ISOS, p. 212.

[53] Idem, Apocalypse, p. 158. See Fasching's book, p. 79.

in Scripture about perdition and the like with objective reality.That is, the warnings really are only a heuristic device. We should not imagine that they will be objectively realized. Thus, warnings about final condemnation have to do only with what Ellul calls "the pedagogy of God."[54]

Last, and most important, in Ellul's high Christology, it is logically impossible and inconceivable that the work of Christ is in any way inconclusive. Where sin has abounded, His grace abounds all the more. It is simply impossible that anyone falls outside the scope of Jesus Christ and His redemption. The existence of any finally unsaved person would constitute a final victory of the powers. According to Ellul, "it is not theologically possible that there be damned men."[55] In the incarnation we have received the "inalienable assurance" that God is with us, that He is for us, that all His judgement has fallen on His Son, and that any exclusion from His work of love in Christ is unimaginable.[56]

Many interpreters have overlooked Ellul's universalism and its importance for his overall thought. From several perspectives it mitigates the consistency of his dialectical method. In the criticisms which follow, we need to keep in mind that what is at issue is not the validity of universalism per se. As far as this work is concerned, that is beside the point. The common denominator of all the following criticisms is that Ellul's universalism creates an internal inconsistency within his dialectical method. Three points are worth noting.

First, Ellul presents his readers with a selective reading of the Biblical texts. He dissolves the obvious tension in Scripture which is seen in the numerous texts which support either the universalistic or particularistic positions. Although in one place he acknowledges the presence of texts

---

[54] Ibid., p. 275.

[55] Ibid., p. 213. Cf. also pages 88, 212. See Gill's book, page 67, on this point.

[56] Idem, Humiliation, p. 56. We should recall Ellul's distinction between the Already and the Not Yet. This final and ultimate triumph of Christ has already been accomplished, but it is not yet fully realized. See Humiliation, pages 81-82. In Apocalypse (p. 112), Ellul writes, "The judgement of the world . . . has been done upon the cross of Jesus Christ; it is a thing already realized, which no longer has need of being done. . . revealed, exerted against Jesus; and he has borne, accepted, assumed that totality."

which would create problems for his universalism,[57] the overwhelming bulk of his writings pays little attention to them. This is quite atypical of Ellul, too, for we have seen how in most cases he is eager to preserve these dialectical tensions in Scripture. In Chapter Two we gave examples of this dialectical hermeneutic which interpreted the Biblical texts on law, the state, money and the world in a way which was consistent with his overall method. When it comes to universalism, though, Ellul does not do justice to the large body of Biblical texts which present the particularistic view of salvation.

Second, we have also seen how important for Ellul is the insistence that people have free wills and that the decisions and choices which they make are of strategic value. According to Ellul, God always and only works through the actions and decisions which people make. He never forces anyone to do anything.[58] And yet, what is universal salvation but the final overpowering act of God in spite of what one may will? It is clear that if universalism is a foregone conclusion, and the final redemptive state of everyone is predetermined, then human actions no longer have ultimate soteriological value. Ellul admits in one place that humankind's eternal peril is not a maximum or final danger, but only a limited one,[59] but he is not ready to admit that this is inconsistent with his method. In two places he addresses the criticism which we are making as a possible flaw,[60] but he does not back down from his position. He would be more consistent with his dialectical method if he maintained and upheld the tension between God's Yes and No in which human actions did have ultimate and not merely penultimate consequences.

Third, another important theme in Ellul is his stress on the importance of the individual. In good Kierkegaardian fashion Ellul would have us return to the vital distinction between the single individual and the collective mass.[61] The

---

[57] See Apocalypse, pp. 275-276.

[58] Ellul, The Politics of God and the Politics of Man, pp. 33-34.

[59] Idem, Jonah, p. 54.

[60] See The Politics of God and the Politics of Man, pp. 190ff., and Apocalypse, p. 112.

[61] Ellul, "Between Chaos and Paralysis," pp. 748-749.

importance of the individual for Ellul's thought is reflected in the common criticism that he has totally neglected the corporate or communal aspects of ethics and theology. Again, he is neither entirely clear nor consistent at this point. On the one hand, he writes that liberation is not a collective matter,[62] while on the other hand he says that in the divine economy of salvation there is a "strict unity in which God holds men collectively" (both for good, salvation, and for ill, for the sin and guilt inherited from the Fall).[63]

Thus, by affirming a universalism in which God grants salvation to all people without discrimination, humankind is treated as a homogeneous mass in which the vital role of the individual is negated. In regard to salvation, people are treated en masse, and all heterogeneity is lost. Ellul is liable for the charge, made by his spiritual ancestor over 100 years ago, of doing away with Christianity by making all people, in the final outcome, Christian.[64] A position more consistent with his method would affirm the ongoing dialectical tension between the single individual and God, between God's Yes of grace and His No of judgement.

Ellul could mitigate the force of these criticisms against his universalism in at least two ways. He could be more explicit about what he implicitly affirms, that his concept of dialectic is limited to history, and that there is no reason for the dialectic to continue after this life. I have found only one place where he hints at such.[65] Second, he could affirm the sort of universalism which John Hick does. For Hick, there is a type of dialectic which continues after history, in which human actions continue to have salvific value (for good or ill) as God lures people to Himself by their own free decisions. Hick takes this position because he recognizes and admits the problems incurred in a view like Ellul's, that is, that it is contradictory to affirm both that people exercise free will and

---

[62] Idem, The Ethics of Freedom, p. 270.

[63] Idem, The Politics of God and the Politics of Man, p. 109.

[64] On this criticism of Ellul's denial of the individual, see Kierkegaard's Attack Upon Christendom, trans. by Walter Lowrie (Princeton: Princeton University Press, 1972), pp. 188-189, and 226; the The Sickness Unto Death, trans. by Howard and Edna Hong (Princeton: Princeton University Press, 1980), pp. 122-124.

[65] Ellul, Humiliation, p. 269.

that salvation is granted to all immediately upon death no matter what. For Hick, the universal salvation of all people is not a logical necessity, as it is for Ellul, but a probability, albeit a probability so likely that he calls it a "practical certainty."[66] Ellul takes neither of these routes, though, and his vigorous affirmation of universalism remains as an inconsistency in his dialectical method.[67]

D. Ellul's Contributions to Theological Method

While people often refer to Ellul as a simple "lay theologian,"[68] readers should keep in mind that this designation can be quite misleading. Ellul commands an exacting knowledge of the history of the church and its theology which rivals that of many "professional" theologians. His theological expertise is second only to his brilliance as a historian and sociologist.[69] A reading of almost any one of his theological or biblical tomes shows that Ellul has done his homework and that one cannot dismiss him as a novice who has strayed from his field of expertise. Ellul has made a genuine contribution to contemporary theology. If Fasching's optimism is exaggerated,[70] Vahanian aptly suggests that the sheer number of responses to Ellul's work shows the seriousness with which scholars are taking his work. [71] It remains for us in these last pages to suggest some of the particular strengths of Ellul's theological method. Three stand out.

---

[66]John Hick, Evil and the God of Love, revised edition (San Francisco: Harper and Row, 1978), p. 344.

[67]For two good presentations of the case against universalism, see J.I. Packer, "Problems of Universal Salvation," Bibliotheca Sacra 130 (January-March): 3-11; and C.S. Lewis, "Hell," Chapter 8 in The Problem of Pain (New York: Macmillan, 1962), pp. 118-128.

[68]See, for example, Berthoud's article, p. 176.

[69]Ellul's magnum opus, Histoire des institutions, vols. 1-5 (Paris: Presses Universitaires de France, 1951-1956), continues to be used as a standard text in French universities.

[70]See footnote #11 of this chapter.

[71]Vahanian, "Jacques Ellul and the Religious Illusion," p. xxxvi.

1. Socrates, Kierkegaard, and Ellul

Scholars often point to the maieutic nature of Kierkegaard's authorship, which itself draws upon the Socratic
method. I would argue that this same characteristic applies to
Ellul as well, in a formal if not material way, and that it
constitutes one of his unique strengths.[72] That is, Ellul
intends not only to inform the reader, but to engage him or her
in a personal dialogue. One of his goals is to force his reader
to interact with him, to make a personal decision about what he
is reading, and, should he disagree with Ellul, to go further
and to do better than Ellul has. The last thing he wants is a
simplistic or uncritical acceptance of his work. As Marty
observes, "there can no more be an 'Ellul Movement' truly
faithful to his thought than there can be a 'Soren Kierkegaard
Club.'"[73]

What Ellul does desire is an audience which will engage his
thought in critical, Socratic dialectic, examine cherished
beliefs, and move forward in new critical awareness. His
deliberate refusal to provide his readers with a blueprint of
solutions or answers for all the problems he raises resides in
this characteristic of his authorship. As he told Menninger in
an interview, the purpose of his work is "to provoke a reaction
of personal reflection, and thus to obligate the reader to
choose for himself a course of action...I don't want disciples,
I don't want people to obey me. I want to incite people."[74]

Two aspects of his method contribute to this particular
strength of Ellul. First, his eclecticism as a generalist adept
in many fields brings to the theological task a breadth and
depth of knowledge which enriches his enterprise. Ellul's
wide-ranging interests invest his works with a freshness which
helps him to formulate old problems in new ways and to see
common themes from different angles. This multifaceted nature
of Ellul's scholarship helps to attract a larger reading
audience than most writers can expect.

Second, Ellul's prophetic apocalypticism permits no
neutrality when reading him. While this is often a disturbing
feature of his writing, it is also a feature which helps him to

---

[72]See footnote #67 of Chapter Two.

[73]Marty, p. 3.

[74]Ellul, to Menninger, in Menninger's dissertation,
p. 217.

accomplish his primary goal of forcing readers to engage him in a dialogue. If readers can get beyond the sometimes irritating style of Ellul to the real content of his books, Ellul will have been at least partially successful. He is anything but boring, and one certainly does not have to agree with him to benefit from him. Like Kierkegaard before him, one of Ellul's primary strengths is his ability to hold his reader's attention, to lure him into a dialectical exchange of ideas, and to move us off of dead center and on to fresh insights.

2. Theology from above and below

Ellul would agree with both Cobb[75] and Ramm[76] that a positive biblical methodology which focuses on Jesus Christ, exemplified best in Barth, still constitutes a viable way in which to do theology today. Those who are amenable to such an orientation will find in Ellul a rich and substantial example of a theology von oben. While this alone would constitute a strength for some, the real contribution which Ellul has made in this regard is his combining with this theology from above a sensitivity for many of the concerns of a theology from below.

On the one hand, Ellul is a thoroughgoing theological positivist and we should not at all imply that he is anything else. Theology is based on revelation, which revelation "comes down."[77] Ellul takes to heart the criticisms which Feuerbach and Marx made on man's religiosity. He adamantly rejects any and all natural theology. The specificity of God's unique revelation in Jesus Christ constitutes theology's starting point. While Ellul does not denigrate human reason, and seeks instead to avoid both rationalistic and irrational abuses, he is clearly in the tradition in which faith seeks understanding. Reason is a guide but not the normative guide for theology. Like Barth, Ellul would affirm that God alone can speak of God, and that theology must begin with His divine self-revelation.

On the other hand, Ellul combines with this approach a sensitivity to many of the concerns of a theology from below. He is anything but a world-denying, Christ-against-culture theologian. In fact, as Vahanian has suggested, in some ways just the opposite is true: Ellul challenges us to embrace the

---

[75]Cobb, p. 320.

[76]Ramm's entire book is addressed to this point.

[77]Ellul, Living Faith, p. 129.

world on both the cognitive and experiential levels.[78] He is quite aware of positive theology's tendency to become other-worldly in the bad sense of that word. For Ellul, that is intolerable. We saw how he criticized Barth's theology at just this point, which theology he considers to be too unrelated to the Sitz im Leben of modern man. Tops on Ellul's agenda for theology is the necessity to correlate and confront, in a mutually critical dialectic, the world and the gospel. We must never separate the two.

As we have seen, Ellul's corpus bears out this concern, with its two tracks of study, one devoted to understanding the modern world, and one devoted to understanding the Scriptures. If Ellul fails to wax eloquent about all the benefits of modern culture, this is because these are obvious to him. He wants to move beyond this and to engage in an active, constructive dialectic between faith and the world. Thus, Ellul is far from the perspective of a Tertullian or a Tolstoy, as Vahanian notes. In fact, for Ellul, without the world there is no faith.[79]

3. Theology's existential relevance

Closely related to this last point is a third strength of Ellul's program. He challenges us to keep in mind that theology must serve a practical, existential or ethical purpose, that of helping the Christian to formulate a unique style of life which impacts the modern world. This does not mean that Ellul reduces Christianity to ethics as, say, Kant did. Far from it. Our point is that he does, though, have a healthy disdain for theology which is nothing more than a purely academic exercise.

We noted in Chapter One that it is not improper to view Ellul as an "existential" thinker. One of theology's greatest dangers is what Tillich called the "detached objectivity" of the philosopher. Ellul would agree with Tillich that the true theologian, unlike the detached philosopher, is involved "with the whole of his existence, with his finitude and his anxiety, with his self-contradictions and his despair, with the healing forces in him and in his social situation. Every theological statement derives its seriousness from these elements of existence."[80]

---

[78]Vahanian, "Jacques Ellul and the Religious Illusion," pp. xv-xviii.

[79]Ibid., p. xviii.

[80]Tillich, p. 23. See footnote #80 of Chapter One.

The final goal of theology revolves around this practical, existential orientation. Purely academic theology bores Ellul. He bemoans the dry and dusty treatises on gnosticism. We should not search the Scriptures for information about God ad intra. This is not its purpose. Ellul's involvement with the reform of theological education in his own denomination illustrates this point. One of his main concerns about ministerial education was that theory and life must confront each other and that merely academic training would produce ill-equipped pastors.[81]

A final strength of Ellul, then, is this eagerness to relate theology to real life, to what Kierkegaard referred to as "the things which matter."[82] What really matters, according to Ellul, is the possibility of hope and freedom in a world of oppression and necessity. If theology loses this "existential" perspective, then it betrays its raison d'etre.

If Ellul is pessimistic about unregenerate people and culture, he is optimistic about the possibilities for a practical, vibrant hope and freedom based upon the gospel. The goal of theology is not to disseminate information but to communicate this hope and freedom to the person in the street. Ellul's work is never what he calls a simple "affair of the intellect," but an attempt to help us "emerge from the blind alley, knowing that this gift has been granted to us."[83] In the gift of Jesus Christ, humankind has the ultimate demonstration that God is with us and for us and that genuine hope and freedom are truly possible. To communicate this is theology's task, and Ellul does it well.

----

[81]Ellul, ISOS, pp. 112-113. Ellul's personal involvement with helping juvenile delinquents also illustrates the point we are making.

[82]Kierkegaard begins The Sickness Unto Death with this prayer: "Herr! gieb uns blöde Augen für Dinge, die nichts taugen, Und Augen voller Klarheit in alle deine Wahrheit."

[83]Ellul, Hope, p. x.

BIBLIOGRAPHY

There are two things to note about this bibliography. First, I have given the English titles when available. Second, Ellul has written far too much for this bibliography to be anything near exhaustive, and, for that reason, I have listed four bibliographies which do, in fact, come close to doing this.

Bibliographies

Fasching, Darrell J. The Thought of Jacques Ellul: A Systematic Exposition. New York: Edwin Mellen Press, 1981, pp. 210-16.

Gill, David W. "Bibliography," in Jacques Ellul: Interpretive Essays, edited by Clifford G. Christians and Jay M. VanHook. Urbana: University of Illinois Press, 1981, pp. 309-328.

_____. The Word of God in the Ethics of Jacques Ellul. Metuchen, N.J.: The Scarecrow Press, 1984, pp. 189-206.

Hanks, Joyce. Research in Philosophy and Technology, Supplement I. Jacques Ellul: A Comprehensive Bibliography. Greenwich, C.T.: JAI Press, 1984.

Primary Resources

1. Books

Ellul, Jacques. Apocalypse: The Book of Revelation. New York: Seabury, 1977.

_____. Autopsy of Revolution. New York: Alfred A. Knopf, 1971.

_____. The Betrayal of the West. New York: Seabury, 1978.

_____. A Critique of the New Commonplaces. New York: Alfred A. Knopf, 1968.

_____. The Ethics of Freedom. Grand Rapids: William B. Eerdmans, 1976.

_____. False Presence of the Kingdom. New York: Seabury, 1972.

147

_____. *Hope in Time of Abandonment*. New York: Seabury, 1973.

_____. *The Humiliation of the Word*. Grand Rapids: William B. Eerdmans, 1985.

_____. *In Season, Out of Season*. San Francisco: Harper and Row, 1982.

_____. *The Judgement of Jonah*. Grand Rapids: William B. Eerdmans, 1971.

_____. *Living Faith: Belief and Doubt in a Perilous World*. San Francisco: Harper and Row, 1983.

_____. *The Meaning of the City*. Grand Rapids: William B. Eerdmans, 1970.

_____. *Money and Power*. Downers Grove, I.L.: Inter-Varsity Press, 1984.

_____. *The New Demons*. New York: Seabury, 1975.

_____. *Perspectives On Our Age*. New York: Seabury, 1981.

_____. *The Political Illusion*. New York: Alfred A. Knopf, 1967.

_____. *The Politics of God and the Politics of Man*. Grand Rapids: William B. Eerdmans, 1972.

_____. *Prayer and Modern Man*. New York: Seabury, 1972.

_____. *The Presence of the Kingdom*. Philadelphia: Westminster, 1951.

_____. *Propaganda: The Formation of Men's Attitudes*. New York: Alfred A. Knopf, 1965.

_____. *La Subversion du christianisme*. Paris: Seuil, 1984.

_____. *The Technological Society*. New York: Alfred A. Knopf, 1964.

_____. *The Technological System*. New York: Continuum, 1980.

_____. *The Theological Foundation of Law*. New York: Seabury, 1969.

_____. *To Will and To Do*. Philadelphia: Pilgrim Press, 1969.

_____. _Violence: Reflections from a Christian Perspective_. New York: Seabury, 1969.

2. Articles

Ellul, Jacques. "L'Antidestin." _Foi et Vie_ 84 (January 1985): 113-122.

_____. "Between Chaos and Paralysis." _The Christian Century_ 85 (June 5, 1968): 747-750.

_____. "The Biology of Technique." _Nation_ (May 24, 1965): 567-568.

_____. "La Blancheur de la liberté." _Réforme_ 1525 (June 8, 1974): 3.

_____. "Conformism and the Rationale of Technique." In _Can We Survive Our Future?_ George Urban and Michael Glenny, eds. New York: St. Martin's Press, 1972, pp. 89-102.

_____. "La Croix et la liberté." _Le Christianisme au XX Siècle_ 11 (March 15, 1982): 5.

_____. "The Cultural and Social Factors Influencing Church Division." _Ecumenical Review_ 4 (April 1952): 269-275.

_____. "Epilogue: On Dialectic." In _Jacques Ellul: Interpretive Essays_. Clifford G. Christians and Jay M. VanHook, eds. Urbana: University of Illinois Press, 1981, pp. 291-308.

_____. "From Jacques Ellul." In _Introducing Jacques Ellul_. James Holloway, ed. Grand Rapids: William B. Eerdmans, 1970, pp. 5-6.

_____. "L'Homme et l'ordinateur." _Evangile et Liberté_ 94.1 (January 7, 1980): 8-9.

_____. "How I Discovered Hope." _The Other Side_ 102 (March 1980): 28-31.

_____. "Karl Barth and Us." _Sojourners_ 7 (December 1978): 22-24.

_____. "La Liberté dénaturée." _Réforme_ 1551 (December 7, 1974): 14-15.

_____. "Lust for Power." _Katallagete_ 7.2 (Fall 1979): 30-33.

_____. "Les Marges de la liberté en Occident." La Vie
Protestante 43 (February 29, 1980): 1-2.

_____. "Mirror of These Ten Years." The Christian Century 87
(February 18, 1970): 200-204.

_____. "Nature, Technique, and Artificiality." In Research in
Philosophy and Technology, Volume 3, Paul T. Durbin, ed.
Greenwich, C.T.: JAI Press, 1980, pp. 263-283.

_____. "La Peur de la liberté." Sud-Ouest Dimanche
(November 4, 1979): 5.

_____. "Pour un socialisme toute autre." Réforme 1977
(March 12, 1983): 7.

_____. "Problems of Sociological Method." Social Research 43
(Spring 1976): 6-24.

_____. "Le Rapport de l'homme à la création selon la Bible."
Foi et Vie 73 (September-December 1974): 137-155. Reprinted
and translated into English in Theology and Technology, Carl
Mitcham and Jim Grote, eds. Washington, D.C.: University
Press of America, 1984.

_____. "Réflexion sur le monde de la nécessité." Vie, Art,
Cité: Revue Suisse Romande, 14th series, no. 1 (1950):
37-39. Signed "Jean Ellul."

_____. "La Responsabilité du christianisme dans la nature et
la liberté." Combat Nature 54 (January-February 1983):
16-17.

_____. "Search for an Image." The Humanist (November-December)
1973): 22-25.

_____. "La Sens de la liberté chez Saint Paul." Foi et Vie 61
(May-June 1962): 3-20.

_____. "Social Change." In Baker's Dictionary of Christian
Ethics, Carl F. H. Henry, ed. Grand Rapids: Baker Book
House, 1973, pp. 629-632.

_____. "La Technique et les premieres chapitres de la
Genèse." Foi et Vie 59 (March-April 1960): 97-113.
Reprinted and translated in Theology and Technology, cited
above.

_____. "Technique, Institutions, and Awareness." The American
Behavioral Scientist 11 (July-August 1968): 38-42.

_____. "The Technological Order." In <u>Philosophy and Tech-</u>
<u>nology: Readings in the Philosophical Problems of</u>
<u>Technology</u>, Carl Mitcham and R. Mackey, eds. New York: John
Wiley and Sons, 1976, pp. 35-47.

_____. "The Technological Revolution and its Moral and
Political Consequences." In <u>Concilium: The Evolving World</u>
<u>and Theology</u>, Johannes B. Metz, ed. New York: Paulist
Press, 1967, pp. 97-107.

_____. "Technology and the Gospel." <u>International Review of</u>
<u>Missions</u> 66 (April 1977): 109-117.

_____. "Unbridled Spirit of Power." <u>Sojourners</u> 11.7-8
(July-August 1982): 12-15.

_____. "Work and Calling." <u>Katallagete</u> 4 (Fall-Winter 1972):
8-16

_____. "'The World' in the Gospels." <u>Katallagete</u> 6 (Spring
1974): 16-23.

<u>Secondary Resources</u>

1. <u>Dissertations and Theses</u>

Bradley, Richard. "The Kingdom of God and Social Change in
the Thought of Jacques Ellul." Th.M. thesis, Princeton
Theological Seminary, 1971.

Burke, John David. "Jacques Ellul: Theologian and Social
Critic." Ph.D. dissertation, Washington State University,
1980.

Fasching, Darrell J. "The Apocalypse of Freedom: Christian
Ethics in the Technological Society. A Defense of the
Social Ethics of Jacques Ellul." Ph.D. dissertation,
Syracuse University, 1978.

Gill, David. "The Word of God in the Ethics of Jacques Ellul."
Ph.D. dissertation, University of Southern California, 1979.

Ihara, Randall Homma. "Redeeming the Time: Theology,
Technology, and Politics in the Thought of Jacques Ellul."
Ph.D. dissertation, University of Tennessee, 1975.

Matheke, David George. "To Will and To Do God's Word: An
Examination of the Christian Meaning of the Works of

Jacques Ellul." D.Div. dissertation, Vanderbilt University Divinity School, 1972.

Menninger, David Charles. "Technique and Politics: The Political Thought of Jacques Ellul." Ph.D. dissertation, University of California, Riverside, 1974.

Miller, Duane Russell. "The Effect of Technology Upon Humanization in the Thought of Lewis Mumford and Jacques Ellul." Ph.D. dissertation, Boston University, 1972.

Mulkey, Robert Cranford. "The Theology of Politics in the Writings of Jacques Ellul." Th.D. dissertation, Southern Baptist Theological Seminary, 1973.

Temple, Katharine Crichton. "The Task of Jacques Ellul: A Proclamation of Biblical Faith as Requisite for Understanding the Modern Project." Ph.D. dissertation, McMaster University, Canada, 1976.

Wren, Gary Paul. "Technique, Society and Politics. A Critical Study of the Work of Jacques Ellul." Ph.D. dissertation, Claremont Graduate School, 1977.

2. Books

Adler, Mortimer. The Idea of Freedom; A Dialectical Examination of the Conceptions of Freedom. Westport, C.T.: Greenwood Press, 1958.

Angeles, Peter. Dictionary of Philosophy. New York: Harper and Row, 1981.

Averill, Lloyd. American Theology in the Liberal Tradition. Philadelphia: Westminster, 1967.

Barth, Karl. Church Dogmatics, 13 volumes. Edinburgh: T & T Clark: 1936-1962.

_____. Evangelical Theology: An Introduction. Grand Rapids: William B. Eerdmans, 1980.

_____. The Theology of Schleiermacher. Dietrich Ritschl, ed. Grand Rapids: William B. Eerdmans, 1982.

Burke, Kenneth. A Grammar of Motives. New York: Meridian, 1962.

Calvin, John. Institutes of the Christian Religion. Philadelphia: Westminster Press, 1960.

Cauthen, Kenneth. The Impact of American Religious Liberalism.
New York: Harper and Row, 1962.

Christians, Clifford G., and VanHook, Jay M., eds. Jacques
Ellul: Interpretive Essays. Urbana: University of
Illinois Press, 1981.

Cobb, John. Living Options in Protestant Theology; A Survey of
Methods. Philadelphia: Westminster Press, 1962.

Cox, Harvey. The Secular City: Secularization and Urbanization
in Theological Perspective. New York: MacMillan, 1966.

Dravasa, Etienne, Claude Emeri, and Jean-Louis Seurin, eds.
Religion, sociétié et politique: Mélanges en hommage à
Jacques Ellul. Paris: Presses Universitaires de France,
1983.

Fasching, Darrell J. The Thought of Jacques Ellul: A Systematic
Exposition. New York: Edwin Mellen Press, 1981.

Ferkiss, Victor. Technological Man: The Myth and the Reality.
New York: Mentor Books, 1969.

Gill, David W. The Word of God in the Ethics of Jacques Ellul.
Metuchen, N.J.: Scarecrow Press, 1984.

Gurvitch, Georges. Dialectique et sociologie. Paris:
Flammarion, 1962.

Hegel, G. F. The Logic of Hegel. Oxford: Clarendon Press,
1892.

Henry, Carl F.H., ed. Baker's Dictionary of Christian Ethics.
Grand Rapids: Baker Book House, 1973.

Hick, John. Evil and the God of Love, revised edition. San
Francisco: Harper and Row, 1978.

Holloway, James, ed. Introducing Jacques Ellul. Grand Rapids:
William B. Eerdmans, 1970.

Hook, Sidney. From Hegel to Marx. London: Victor Gollanez,
1936.

Käsemann, Ernest. Jesus Means Freedom. Philadelphia: Fortress
Press, 1977.

Kaufmann, Gordon D. _An Essay in Theological Method_. Missoula, M.T.: Scholars Press, 1975.

Kierkegaard, Soren. _Attack Upon "Christendom."_ Princeton: Princeton University Press, 1968.

_____. _The Concept of Anxiety_. Princeton: Princeton University Press, 1980.

_____. _Concluding Unscientific Postscript_. Princeton: Princeton University Press, 1941.

_____. _Either/Or_. 2 vols. Princeton: Princeton University Press, 1943.

_____. _Fear and Trembling and Repetition_. Princeton: Princeton University Press, 1983.

_____. _For Self-Examination and Judge For Yourselves!_ Princeton: Princeton University Press, 1941.

_____. _Philosophical Fragments_. Princeton: Princeton University Press, 1974.

_____. _The Point of View for My Work as an Author. A Report to History_. New York: Harper and Row, 1962.

_____. _The Present Age_. New York: Harper and Row, 1962.

_____. _Purity of Heart is to Will One Thing_. New York: Harper and Row, 1956.

_____. _The Sickness Unto Death_. Princeton: Princeton University Press, 1980.

_____. _Training in Christianity_. Princeton: Princeton University Press, 1944.

Koenker, Ernest. _Great Dialecticians in Modern Christian Thought_. Minneapolis: Augsburg Publishing House, 1971.

Kuhns, William. _The Post-Industrial Prophets_. New York: Weybright and Talley, 1971.

Lewis, C.S. _The Problem of Pain_. New York: MacMillan, 1962.

Metz, Johannes. _The Evolving World and Theology_. New York: Paulist Press, 1967.

Mitcham, Carl, and Robert Mackey, eds. Philosophy and Technology. Readings in the Philosophical Problems of Technology. New York: MacMillan, 1972.

Moltmann, Jürgen. Theology of Hope. New York: Harper and Row, 1967.

Mumford, Lewis. Technics and Civilization. New York: Harcourt, Brace, and World, 1934.

Niebuhr, H. Richard. Christ and Culture. New York: Harper and Row, 1951.

Oden, Thomas. Agenda for Theology. San Francisco: Harper and Row, 1979.

Pannenberg, Wolfhart. Theology and the Philosophy of Science. Philadelphia: Westminster Press, 1976.

Ramm, Bernard. After Fundamentalism: The Future of Evangelical Theology. New York: Harper and Row, 1983.

Rauschenbusch, Walter. A Theology for the Social Gospel. Nashville: Abingdon, 1981.

Rescher, Nicholas. Dialectics: A Controversy-Oriented Approach to the Theory of Knowledge. Albany: State University of New York Press, 1977.

Robinson, James, ed. The Beginnings of Dialectical Theology. Richmond: John Knox Press, 1968.

Schuurman, Egbert. Reflections on the Technological Society. Toronto: Wedge Publishing Society, 1977.

Sontag, Frederick. A Kierkegaard Handbook. Atlanta: John Knox Press, 1979.

Stanley, Manfred. The Technological Conscience: Survival and Dignity in an Age of Expertise. New York: Free Press, 1978.

Sykes, Stephen. The Identity of Christianity: Theologians and the Essence of Christianity from Schleiermacher to Barth. Philadelphia: Fortress Press, 1984.

Taylor, Mark. Deconstructing Theology. New York: Crossroad Publishing Company and Scholars Press, 1982.

Tillich, Paul. Systematic Theology, 3 vols. Chicago: University of Chicago Press, 1951-1963.

Tucker, Robert C. The Marx-Engels Reader, second edition. New York: W.W. Norton and Co., 1978.

Young, Robert. Analytical Concordance to the Bible, 22nd edition. New York: Funk and Wagnalls, n.d.

William, Daniel Day. God's Grace and Man's Hope. New York: Harper and Brothers, 1949.

3. Articles

Badertscher, John. "George P. Grant and Jacques Ellul on Freedom in the Technological Society." In George Grant in Process: Essays and Conversations. Larry Schmidt, ed. Toronto: House of Anansi, 1978, pp. 79-89.

Berthoud, Jean-Marc. "Jacques Ellul et l'impossible dialectique entre Marx et Calvin." La Revue Réformée 33.4 (1982): 176-191.

Boli-Bennett, John. "The Absolute Dialectics of Jacques Ellul." In Research in Philosophy and Technology, vol. 3, cited above, pp. 171-201.

Bouillard, Henri. "Dialectical Theology." In Sacramentum Mundi, vol. II. New York: Herder and Herder, 1968, p. 78.

Bromiley, Geoffrey. "Barth's Influence on Jacques Ellul." In Jacques Ellul: Interpretive Essays, cited above, pp. 32-51.

Brown, Norman O. "Jacques Ellul: Beyond Geneva and Jerusalem." Democracy 2.4 (Fall 1982): 119-126.

Christians, Clifford G. "Ellul On Solution: An Alternative but no Prophecy." In Jacques Ellul: Interpretive Essays, cited above, pp. 147-173.

Cérézuelle, Daniel. "From the Technological Phenomenon to the Technological System." In Research in Philosophy and Technology, vol. 3, cited above, pp. 161-170.

Cox, Harvey. "The Ungodly City: A Theological Response to Jacques Ellul." Commonweal 94 (July 9, 1971): 351-357.

DeKoster, Lester. Review of The Meaning of the City. Banner (July 16, 1971): 24-25.

Dollen, Charles. Review of Hope in Time of Abandonment. Best
Sellers 33.7 (July 1, 1973): 162.

Eller, Vernard. "A Voice on Vocation: The Contribution of
Jacques Ellul." The Reformed Journal 29 (May 1979): 16-21.

_____. "Ellul and Kierkegaard: Closer Than Brothers." In
Jacques Ellul: Interpretive Essays, cited above, pp. 52-66.

_____. "Four Who Remember: Kierkegaard, the Blumhardts, Ellul
and Muggeridge." Katallagete 3 (Spring 1971): 6-12.

_____. "How Jacques Ellul Reads the Bible." The Christian
Century (November 29, 1972): 1212-1215.

_____. "The Polymath Who Knows Only One Thing." Brethren Life
and Thought 18 (Spring 1973): 77-84.

Gill, David. "Activist and Ethicist: Meet Jacques Ellul."
Christianity Today (September 10, 1976): 1220-1222.

_____. "Biblical Theology of the City." International Standard
Bible Encyclopedia. Grand Rapids: William B. Eerdmans,
1979, revised edition, vol. 1, pp. 713-715.

_____. "Foreword." In Jacques Ellul, Money and Power. Downers
Grove, I.L.: Inter-Varsity Press, 1984, pp. 5-8.

_____. "Introduction." In Jacques Ellul, Living Faith: Belief
and Doubt in a Perilous World. San Francisco: Harper and
Row, 1983, pp. xi-xvi.

_____. "Introduction to the American Edition." In Jacques
Ellul, In Season, Out of Season. San Francisco: Harper
and Row, 1982, pp. v-xii.

_____. "Jacques Ellul and Francis Schaeffer: Two Views of
Western Civilization." Fides et Historia 13.2
(Spring-Summer 1981): 23-37.

_____. "Jacques Ellul: The Prophet as Theologian." Themelios
7.1 (September 1981): 4-14.

_____. Jacques Ellul's View of Scripture." Journal of the
Evangelical Theological Society 25.4 (December 1982):
467-478.

_____. "Prophet in the Technological Wilderness." Catholic
Agitator (October 1976): 3-4.

157

_____. Review of Jacques Ellul, Subversion du christianisme, Fides et Historia XVII, No. 2 (Spring-Summer 1985): 70-77.

_____. "A Study in Contrasts: Bennett and Ellul." Radix 8 (July-August 1976): 6.

Gorman, William. "Jacques Ellul: A Prophetic Voice." The Center Magazine 1 (October-November 1967): 34-37.

Hall, Roland. "Dialectics." In The Encyclopedia of Philosophy, 1972 reprint edition, pp. 385-389.

Hanks, Thomas. "How Ellul Transcends Liberation Theologies." TSF Bulletin (September-October 1984): 13-16.

_____. "Jacques Ellul: The Original Liberation Theologian." TSF Bulletin (May-June 1984): 8-11.

Heddendorf, Russell. "The Christian World of Jacques Ellul." Christian Scholar's Review 2, no. 4 (1973): 291-307.

Hollenbach, David. Review of The Ethics of Freedom. Theological Studies 37, no. 4 (December 1976): 708-710.

Holmes, Arthur. "On Pushing a Prophet." Reformed Journal 32, no. 11 (November 1982): 8.

_____. "A Philosophical Critique of Ellul on Natural Law." In Jacques Ellul: Interpretive Essays, cited above, pp. 229-250.

Hook, Sidney. "The Philosophy of Dialectical Materialism, I." Journal of Philosophy 25, no. 5 (March 1, 1928): 113-124.

_____. "The Philosophy of Dialectical Materialism, II." Journal of Philosophy 25, no. 6 (March 15, 1928): 141-155.

_____. "What is Dialectic? I." Journal of Philosophy 26, no. 4 (February 14, 1929): 85-99.

_____. "What is Dialectic? II." Journal of Philosophy 26, no. 5 (February 28, 1929): 113-123.

Konyndyk, Kenneth. "Violence." In Jacques Ellul: Interpretive Essays, cited above, pp. 251-268.

Lasch, Christopher. "The Social Thought of Jacques Ellul." In Introducing Jacques Ellul, cited above, pp. 63-90.

Lavroff, Dmitri Georges. "Avant-propros." In Religion, sociétié, et politique: Mélanges en hommage à Jacques Ellul, cited above, pp. ix-x.

Lescaze, Marie-Claire. "Les Marges de la liberté en Occident. Une Interview de Jacques Ellul." La Vie Protestante 43, no. 8/2 (February 29, 1980): 1-2.

McGreevy, Brian. "Ellul and the Supreme Court on Freedom." Christian Legal Society Quarterly 4, nos. 2-3 (1983): 26-31.

MacIntyre, Alasdair. "Existentialism." In Encyclopedia of Philosophy, 1972 reprint edition, pp. 147-154.

Marty, Martin. "Introduction: Creative Misuses of Jacques Ellul." In Jacques Ellul: Interpretive Essays, cited above, pp. 3-13.

Menninger, David C. "Jacques Ellul: A Tempered Profile." Review of Politics 37 (April 1975): 235-246.

Michaud-Quantin, P. and J. A. Weisheipl. "Dialectics in the Middle Ages." In The New Catholic Encyclopedia, vol. IV. Washington, D.C.: The Catholic University of America, 1967, pp. 846-849.

Minnema, Theodore. "Evil in the Thought of Jacques Ellul." Reformed Journal 23 (May-June 1973): 17-20.

Mondin, B. "Dialectic in Theology." In The New Catholic Encyclopedia, cited above, p. 842.

Packer, J.I. "Problems of Universal Salvation." Bibliotheca Sacra 130 (January-March 1973): 3-11.

Pickrel, Paul. "Heading Toward Postcivilization (Boulder, Berkner, Ellul, Snow, Murdoch, Bellow)." Harper's Magazine 229 (October 1964): 122-128.

Popper, Karl. "What is Dialectic?" Mind: A Quarterly Review of Psychology and Philosophy 49, no. 196 (October 1940): 401-426.

Punzo, Vincent. "Jacques Ellul on the Presence of the Kingdom in a Technological Society." Logos (University of Santa Clara, CA), vol. 1 (1980): 125-137.

Riemer, Neal. "The Future of the Democratic Revolution: Toward A More Prophetic Politics." Humanities in Society (Fall 1983): 5-18.

Ross, Edward. "The Sociologist in the Role of the Prophet." American Sociological Review 8 (February 1943): 10-14.

Schaar, John H. "Jacques Ellul: Between Babylon and the New Jerusalem." Democracy 2.4 (Fall 1982): 102-118.

Schickel, Richard. "Marx is Dead." Harper's Magazine 244 (April 1972): 96-101.

Sullivan, Robert, and Alfred DiMaio. "Jacques Ellul: Toward Understanding His Political Thinking." Journal of Church and State 24, no. 1 (Winter 1982): 13-28.

Taubes, Jacob. "Dialectic and Analogy." Journal of Religion 34 (April 1954): 111-119.

_____. "On the Nature of Theological Method: Some Reflections on the Methodological Principle of Tillich's Theology." Journal of Religion 34 (January 1954): 12-25.

_____. "Theodicy and Theology. A Philosophical Analysis of Karl Barth's Dialectical Theology." Journal of Religion 34 (October 1954): 231-243.

Temple, Katharine. "The Sociology of Jacques Ellul." In Research in Philosophy and Technology, vol. 3, cited above, pp. 223-261.

Vahanian, Gabriel. "Jacques Ellul and the Religious Illusion." In The Thought of Jacques Ellul: A Systematic Exposition, cited above, pp. xv-xxxviii.

_____. "Technology, Politics, and the Christian Faith." In Introducing Jacques Ellul, cited above, pp. 51-62.

VanHook, Jay M. "The Burden of Jacques Ellul." Reformed Journal 26 (December 1976): 13-17.

Walters-Bugbee, Christopher. "The Politics of Revelation; Jacques Ellul's Approach: Confrontation and Obedience." Sojourners 6, no. 6 (June 1977): 5-8.

Wilson, H.T. "The Sociology of Apocalypse: Jacques Ellul's Reformation of Reformation Thought." Human Context 7, no. 3 (1975): 474-494.

Ziegler, J.J. "Dialectics." In The New Catholic Encyclopedia, cited above, pp. 843-846.

NAME INDEX

161

AUTHOR	PAGE(S)
Dollen, Charles	19
Dravasa, Etienne	1
Eller, Vernard	14, 18, 26, 124
Emeri, Claude	1
Fasching, Darrell J.	2, 3, 4, 11, 12, 19, 22, 61, 82, 83, 86, 92, 98, 123, 124, 137, 141
Ferkiss, Victor	4
Gill, David W.	11, 12, 14, 17, 18, 20, 21, 22, 23, 38, 50, 51, 62, 73, 92, 100, 104, 109, 110, 111, 112, 124, 127, 130, 138
Gorman, William	20, 23
Gurvitch, Georges	34, 41, 54, 135
Hall, Roland	30
Hall, Rupert	22
Hanks, Joyce	2, 23, 27, 44, 68, 124
Hanks, Thomas	3, 4, 19, 27, 95, 96
Heddendorf, Russell	6, 7
Hegel, G. F.	25, 29, 33, 34, 35, 37, 38, 44, 46, 54, 135
Henry, Carl F.H.	70
Hick, John	140, 141
Hollenbach, David	25
Holloway, James	1, 3, 7
Holmes, Arthur	24
Hook, Sidney	30, 31, 33
Ihara, Randall Homma	3, 5, 7, 22